To Julie,

Heree to your
growth!

The 5 Catalysts of 7 Figure Growth

The 5 Catalysts of 7 Figure Growth

by Andy Birol

CAREER
PRESS

Franklin Lakes, NJ

THE 5 CATALYSTS OF 7 FIGURE GROWTH
EDITED AND TYPESET BY ASTRID DERIDDER
Cover design by Cheryl Cohan Finbow
Printed in the U.S.A. by Book-mart Press

To order this title, please call toll-free 1-800-CAREER-1 (NJ and Canada: 201-848-0310) to order using VISA or MasterCard, or for further information on books from Career Press.

Disclaimer: While events and individuals inspire the anonymous examples in this book, no direct or indirect connection to real situations or owners is intended.

The Career Press, Inc., 3 Tice Road, PO Box 687,
Franklin Lakes, NJ 07417
www.careerpress.com

Library of Congress Cataloging-in-Publication Data

Birol, Andy
The 5 catalysts of 7 figure growth : propel your business to the next level / by Andy Birol.
    p. cm.
  Includes index.
  ISBN 1-56414-828-9 (paper)
    1. Industrial management. 2. Business planning. I. Title: Five catalysts of seven figure growth. II. Title.

HD31.B4976 2006
658.4'01—dc22

2005052650

Dedication

This book is dedicated to my daughter
Margo, who has taught me more
about growth than anyone.

Acknowledgments

Writing this book has given me the opportunity to summarize a life's worth of effort, learning, and accomplishments, and I'd like to thank two groups of folks. First, those who actually helped me on this book:

- Alan Weiss, my mentor, whose pushing me to write this book made it happen.

- Lisa Allen Marshall and Astrid deRidder, my editors, who helped me take my lifetime of work and turn it into what you will read.

- Jeff Herman, my agent, whose perseverance resulted in this book being published.

- Carolyn Berg, my virtual assistant, whose support made me able to focus on completing my work.

- Career Press, particularly Michael Pye and Michael Lewis, whose confidence in helping this author become published has enabled you to read this book.

Next, I'd like to thank some folks who helped me get to the point where this book could be written. Without Bob Fruchter, Rebecca Morgan, Rand Curtiss, Shari

Goldstein, Ryan Gerber, Rob Felber, Michael Cannon, my friend Cameron Virrill, and the early influences of Andrew Thomas and Linda Seivertsen, this book would not have come to fruition. Finally, I'd like to thank some people whose profound influence brought me from survival, through confidence, and towards success. They are:

- My parents, Masti and Jackie Birol, whose genes, love, support, and example took me from a child who refused to write to someone who now likes to write.

- My uncle, Ibrahim Acar, whose early influence in Turkey exposed me to entrepreneurship, scholarship, and the love that he gave and showed in so many ways.

- My track and cross-country coach, Shelly Lifton, who found me throwing rocks at school windows in sixth grade and turned me into an All County cross-country runner, teaching me the value of self-sufficiency and hard work.

- Dr. Bruce Coggin, who, in selecting me as a Kemper Scholar, not only allowed me to finish college but provided me with the work experience and exposure to corporate America that started my career.

- My beloved Boston University marketing professor, Dr. Allen Beckwith, who exposed me to a field that he loved and loved teaching, preparing me for my career and my Best and Highest Use.

- My first boss, Dale Stahl, at Union Camp, whose patience and leadership taught me how to succeed in the corporate environment and gave me the opportunity to develop my first products.

- My classmates, teachers, and co-workers at the Kellogg School and at the Management Analysis Center, who surrounded me with extreme academic excellence, scholarship, and intellect.

- Mr. Githongo, of Githongo and Company, who taught me how to build, sustain, and protect a business in the extreme environment of Nairobi, Kenya.

- Mr. Wayne Willis, my boss at VoiceTel, who is also a client and good friend, and whose passion for nurturing new ideas gave birth to many companies that I've been in and around.

- My wife, Joan, whose perseverance, dedication, and commitment to her job, our child, and me, is an inspiration.

- And finally, my 300 clients and the thousands of business owners I have spoken to, whose faith and investment in me has taught me what I needed to know to write this book.

Contents

Foreword

Somewhere around the turn of the millennium, people started calling me a business owner, as opposed to someone who was "consulting" or "starting a business" or "out on his own." I felt honored. Having broken away from the corporate world, I had been accepted into the greatest yet most solitary fraternity in the world: business owners.

I bet you understand. When people find out we own businesses, don't their eyes often shine? The first eager question is usually, "So, what is your business?" Once we tell them, their responses vary depending on whether they want to sell us something, assume we are wealthy, or need a job. But the gleam in their eyes typically remains.

Business owner. The phrase has a certain aura, a sparkle of achievement. Whether you are a sole proprietor, a Mom and Pop shop, a local or regional manufacturer, or the leader of a nationally recognized company, as a business owner you are living the American Dream that escapes most people. Business ownership is about freedom, choice, and personal victory over risk and control. So I ask you: if we owners are living the American Dream, why do so many of our businesses fall short of our expectations?

Let's face it, anyone can set up shop and proclaim himself a business owner. With few exceptions, we owners are not qualified by anyone but our own self-confidence. We are unlicensed and need no certification, not even a college degree. While the great heroes—Henry Ford, Fred Smith, and Bill Gates, for example—shine, most others survive, fail, or struggle to keep hope alive until the next loan payment, customer order, or supplier's credit terms. Running our own firms is an equal-opportunity pathway to great respect and achievement, or to embarrassment, regret, and failure.

Owners know this. Psychologically, it's a pretty clear fork in the road. As Yogi Berra said, "When you come to a fork in the road, take it!" The trouble is, how do we know which path leads to success and which leads to a cliff? The stakes are so high that as owners we tend to creep along an inch at a time, or, even worse, simply stand still. Change involves risk. The status quo becomes set in stone. And we are great at rationalizing: *This is how we've always done it.* If a business isn't growing, however, it's falling behind.

I see scores of owners who subsist in a kind of purgatory I call *Dead Firm Walking*. There is the extremely talented freelancer who is content with just surviving; the scion of the family business whose ambition is trampled beneath the rush and clutch of greedy relatives; the owners who are insecure, or who lack critical resources and the conviction to secure them. Then there are the over-prideful, for whom taking the business to the next level—or any level—represents a loss of purity, as they see themselves "selling out." Finally, there are owners of successful firms who have hit the Peter Principle; they can't admit that the business needs more than their present leadership can provide.

We owners have all of the tools and certainly all of the incentive to grow our businesses, our national economy, and parts of the developing world. New problems demand new solutions. Because I live in Ohio, many of my clients are located in the Rust Belt, which is a little like fighting from the trenches in World War I—so many owners are so focused on not getting shot that they have yet to peek up from the mud. Once dependent on the now-embattled industries of rubber and steel, the region lags behind the rest of the country in transforming itself into a New Economy player. But guess what? Some companies are growing. Many are thriving, in fact, and the winners aren't all service providers. In this book you will read about manufacturers who have transformed their companies to keep pace with foreign competition. They highlight both the need for, and the potential of, companies to be reinvented. The question is *how?*

For most businesses, the tendency toward inertia is reversible if the owner is willing to seek help and make changes. After years of consulting with hundreds of owners, I knew it was time to write a book about the key steps to growth. This isn't a new topic. Yet, while so many MBA entrepreneurial programs, large consulting firms, and companies interested in serving entrepreneurs address the clinical needs of a business, they neglect to explore the profound impact an owner's attitude, beliefs, and level of confidence have on his or her business.

The book you are reading is not the book I would have written 10 years ago, before my own business grew. I came to consulting after many productive years in the corporate world, where I honed my skill set; gained critical knowledge particularly in sales, marketing, and the politics of business; and pushed around enough symbolic paper clips to know I am not cut from the corporate cloth. Despite the vast resources of my employers, and despite great talent in the upper ranks of management, very little got done. Stuff didn't happen—it just sat around. Endless meetings and lunches and reports and strategic analyzing led to—more meetings, lunches, reports, and strategic analyses. I worked for good people. Why, then, did we accomplish so little? Was there something in the water cooler? Was it politics? The collective, competing wills of an entire tier of managers each committed to being the last person on the island?

Once I began running my own show and my means were finally, irrevocably connected to my ends, the answer became clear. My employer companies were guided by corporate stewards who simply lacked the passion, conviction, and financial stake in the business. Those early months contained enough surprises to convince me that I was orbiting a whole new galaxy from the corporate stratosphere I had known. What I had thought would be difficult—drumming up clients and convincing them that my services were worth actual money—proved to be the easiest part of my new job. The trouble came, ironically, in my former area of expertise, database management. I became so mired in time-consuming and ill-conceived administrative functions that I hardly had time to service the new clients that were proving so easy to find. To save my business, I had to redesign my billing practices and delegate the administrative tasks in order to focus on what I did best: helping companies grow.

These experiences taught me three crucial points about business ownership. First, companies either grow or they are sold. Sometimes they go to someone else who grows them, and sometimes into bankruptcy, where they are salvaged for whatever value they can offer to creditors. Second, nothing can stand between an owner and his or her business. There are no obstacles between what we want and what the business is capable of doing, *if we are truly committed to making it happen.* The business succeeds (or fails) on the strength (or weakness) of our sense of purpose, our drive to succeed, and our level of commitment. Third, I learned that every entrepreneur carries a unique skill set, similar to an amateur golfer (I plead guilty) who caddies his own clubs, only some of which leverage his strengths. You may hit onto the green in two, but if you keep three-putting a par-four you won't be winning any trophies. The baggage a person has while in the corporate world will not magically disappear once he hangs out his shingle. Someone with poor people-management skills will still have a hard time dealing with people as a business owner. A chronically disorganized employee will become a chronically disorganized owner.

To succeed, we owners must possess great passion and purpose, but these are not enough to sustain a business beyond its early successes. As owners, in other words, we shoulder both the opportunity and the obligation for controlling our firm's destiny. Owners with passion but little direction often become paralyzed by their desire to do everything right, or flail around in so many directions that the company is eventually pulled apart. Owners who are all direction with no passion breed passive subservience throughout their firm. Avoiding failure does not equal succeeding, as competitors focused on excellence will prove. And owners who lack both conviction and knowledge of how to deliver tangible benefits for their customers are kidding themselves—and everyone around them—about running a business.

Remember Y2K? The fever pitch of worrying that somehow our computer's clock would stop the business world created an entire industry with perhaps the shortest life cycle in history—eighteen months. But its impact was far greater. The management attention, passion, and money poured into this boondoggle could have been put into product development, Internet applications, and customer service. "But nooo!" as Steve Martin would say. We had to fix Y2K! Meanwhile, young sales people were never taught how to be more than order takers in a booming economy. Recruiters chased aging COBOL programmers who milked employers for every cent they could. Business owners were only distracted further.

What if we could have stayed focused? How many of us could keep a clear sense of which customers to serve, why those customers would buy, and what made our companies unique? Here's an answer. By the time the economic recovery took hold in 2004, hundreds of distracted businesses were out of business, and probably several million were hunkered down, too anxious to take bold steps and seize the day. All this during a time when interest rates made money almost free and technology workers were available in droves!

The cost of FUD (Fear, Uncertainty, and Doubt) on our businesses and economy is profound. It suffocates the business owner's ability to grow. True business growth is a natural consequence of excellence. If in doubt, we must peel our company onion down to its essence: *real* customers with *real* problems must spend *real* money to purchase *real* products or services his company *really* makes which solve *real* pain or create *real* opportunity *real* soon. Everything else is a distraction. There is nothing virtual about this reality!

Doesn't this seem like an obvious point? Yet examples of businesses that "just don't get it" abound. Some of these firms are near death, while others are outwardly successful, but all share a set of symptoms:

- The owner is ambivalent and conflicted.
- The company isn't in touch with it's value.
- The company squanders its best opportunities for growth by failing to sell what customers most want or need.
- Customers are partially satisfied and understandably fickle. They will keep buying only until finding a better competitor.

Too many businesses change only when they hurt. As long as minimal growth is acceptable, changing seems risky. If our attitude toward growth is conflicted, our firms will struggle with how to find, keep, and grow more customers. Thus we squander time, energy, and money instead of asking the hard questions.

This book is written for owners and their managers and advisors who want to grow their companies in a more consistent, efficient manner. The PACER Process (Process for Acquiring Customers and Enhancing Retention) I have developed takes the guess work and frustration out of business growth by supplying a duplicable system owners can apply at each stage of growth, from starting out to achieving higher levels of sales and finally to creating a legacy and transitioning the company into the hands of a successor. By applying the same core principles (the five catalysts) and modifying them for each successive milestone (seven-figure growth) you can create and repeat a cycle of organic growth.

The 5 Catalysts of 7 Figure Growth is divided into two sections. The first five chapters present each catalyst in detail to give you a solid understanding of the role it plays in creating business success. In the second section of the book, which begins with Chapter 6, you can apply each catalyst to different phases of growth. I encourage you to read the first section to understand the critical nature of the five catalysts. Then you will be able to launch into the final chapters to examine where you have been, where you are going next, and what actions you must take to drive your company to the next level.

Throughout the book, you'll see a special icon reminding you to turn to the Appendix, where you'll find the Owner's Exercise Series to help you grow your business. These exercises are specially designed to help you clarify and quantify your business growth.

So, owners, start your engines. Yours is the opportunity to mold your business into a unique projection and extension of all that you are and all that your company can do. This is where the fun begins!

Section 1

The 5 Catalysts of 7 Figure Growth

It is my conviction that an owner's drive, passion, and potential carve out the future of his or her company. This concept is hard for some owners to accept, in that anything that is wrong with their "baby"—no matter how old or independent it becomes—is all their fault. To the contrary! When you truly grasp that your firm's success is an outgrowth of your passion, conviction, and drive, you feel the power of your position. No longer must you stress out over the things you can't control—a competitor trying to steal your best customers; a marketing slogan getting poor results; the customer retention software that keeps letting you down—because there is so much you *can* control.

As you will see in Chapters 1 and 2, by deepening your conviction you can discover (or recover) how your particular passions and talents translate into unique solutions for your customers. This is what I call Best and Highest Use®. By pursuing what you love and do well, you can target customers who most need your talents, meet their specific needs, and build loyalty through excellence. The beauty of Best and Highest Use, or BHU, is that it allows you to clarify your goals and simplify your decisions. It is your guide to the actions you must take. Why fret about a competitor targeting your customers? Instead, deepen your relationships with those customers to ensure they stay with your firm.

Following Chapters 1 and 2, of conviction and BHU, are three chapters which turn this pair of concepts into tangible actions you can take to create profitable growth. Chapter 3 provides you with a simple system to find, keep, and growh customers. In Chapter 4 you will learn how to best deliver your BHU. Section one concludes with Chapter 5, where you will learn ways to repeatedly profit from what and how you deliver. five catalysts, each one building on the last, are your path to growth. Read each chapter and then turn to the Appendix for worksheets you can use to clarify your business growth. So let's get started!

Don't forget! When you see this icon, turn to the Appendix for an exercise to help you grow your business...

Chapter 1

From Apprehension to Conviction: How an owner's mindset drives the firm's growth

In these divisive times of blue and red states, beginning with a political example is up there with telling religious or sexual jokes to people you don't know—you'd better be sure the punch line is worth the likely offense! But this chapter is about conviction—and I'm willing to show mine. (Plus, the example is too obvious to pass up.)

Whatever your political leanings, there is no debate about George W. Bush's convictions. The world has witnessed Bush's transformation ever since that awful moment in September 2001 when Andrew Card walked into a Florida classroom and whispered "A second plane hit the towers. We are under attack." Call it a rise to heroism, a reasonable response to terror, or a reactive overreaching of foreign policy—whatever your perspective, Bush's presidency embodies the power of conviction. This point was made again in his approach to the second Gulf War. Picture the scene: a darkened backdrop, the President striding down a long walkway, standing resolute behind the podium. The country was at war. Whether he had debated policy, questioned reports, or reconciled opposing views was, at the time, irrelevant. His mind was made up.

We'll let pundits, historians, and bloggers debate the wisdom of what happened next. The point is this: a leader who, by most assessments, had been drifting through his first nine months of office answered his wake-up call. He responded from the gut—the core of his most deeply held beliefs—and steered world history down a whole new path.

Unfortunately, George W. Bush (like millions of business owners) can have a defining point one year and need another one again the next. During Hurricane Katrina, just when the country needed a leader and a healer, the impact of Michael Brown and FEMA's mismanagement could not be overcome, despite Bush's repeated trips to New Orleans. It is important to remember that defining points themselves don't last forever and owners who have had one are often the first to recognize when they need another.

Okay, you're not the leader of the free world, but you do control your own destiny, a power both exhilarating and terrifying. (Ever have days when you think, "I wouldn't work for any company that would have me as its owner"?) This is why conviction is critical. It is a deeply felt confidence in yourself—your own beliefs, abilities, and power to make decisions—and toward your business. Truly successful leaders possess great confidence and personal conviction. With it, you can overcome almost any adversity.

I know it's around here somewhere

Remember this United Airlines commercial? The scene: a dimly lit boardroom. The characters: men and women hunched around a conference table. The action: the leader striding to the head of the table. He stands, silhouetted in weak light from the window, and solemnly announces that the company's very first customer is now buying from a competitor. Why? Because that customer, the one who believed in the business before anyone else did, no longer feels appreciated.

The room then deflates. The leader passes out airline tickets, commanding his managers to visit each and every client. Heads shake in frustration; groans rise. Then one bold (foolhardy?) soul calls out, "So, what are *you* going to do while we're all out on the road?" The owner doesn't blink. "I'm going to visit an old friend I have neglected for far too long."

Though it aired several years ago, this commercial haunts me. I see the same thing happen with my clients. The owner is humbled but decisive, and his resolve wins our respect. Yet, I have to wonder: how many client messages did he forget to return? How many times did he bite his tongue while his subordinates pursued their own goals ahead of their customers' needs? Why did he let his company drift so far from its customers?

The stern guy in the commercial isn't a real business owner (he plays one on TV) but he represents thousands of men and women who find their companies in crisis despite their sacrifices of time, money, and labor. Many don't know what hit them. Toiling over daily tasks and details, they don't see other companies outperforming their own. When they finally notice, they work even harder, throwing themselves into the same old tasks with renewed fervor. Things get worse. Deep down, these owners know they must fix things, but they're afraid of doing the *wrong* thing. The result is a peculiar lethargy in which the person at the top, the owner, impedes the very success he or she desires.

Here are some examples:

- A computer hardware business loses sales to mass merchandisers despite providing "free service." The owner acknowledges his customers would pay for service but never charges them.
- The owner of an industrial cleaning company won't invest in marketing despite frequent sales slumps. Year after year, he would rather complain than take action.
- A metal shop owner who is losing ground to offshore manufacturers denies that innovation is necessary or even possible. He degrades the progress of his competitors, ultimately pretending that their success doesn't exist!

These owners aren't just stubborn or out of touch—they are paralyzed by ambivalence and self-doubt. They have lost the exhilaration they once felt in serving their customers. Their companies won't grow because they don't believe strongly enough in what their business produces or provides and what they must do to achieve their goals.

Why does this happen? In the corporate world, ambivalence results when the people in charge protect their own assets at the expense of driving excellence throughout their firm. Hierarchy and propriety are valued; creativity is seen as disruptive. These executives lose touch with customers and suppliers, diversify into areas that weaken their core business, and end up forgetting why they're in business in the first place.

But owners are different. We *are* our business. We are the passion, the conviction, and the commitment and, in some cases, even the product! Our companies are the tangible representation of our egos; if we don't believe in what we do, why should anyone else? Ambivalence, for business owners, is more than uncertainty. It is a cancer that, if left unchecked, will invade every cell of our being.

"But Andy," you may be thinking, "I *want* to succeed!" Well, sure— you picked up this book, after all. But the humbled owner from the United Airlines commercial "wanted" to succeed, too.

Don't hedge those bets

Years ago, during the marriage ceremony of a friend of mine, the priest told a story I will never forget. He recounted the 75th wedding anniversary of a couple and the exchange that occurred between the wife and a young single woman. "I'd give anything to have the marriage you did" gushed the young woman, to which the elderly wife sighed, "I *did.*"

Call me old-fashioned, but marriage isn't meant to be a "try and see if you like it" arrangement—that's called cohabitation. Anyone who weds with the intention of backing out later if things don't "work out" is never really married. Things, after all, don't work themselves out; people have to make things work out. In the same way, an owner who "tries out" a business is as committed to that company as I am to my socks. At the first sign of wear, it's time to pull out.

True conviction requires absolute commitment, which means throwing away any personal tendencies toward equivocation. This conviction generates tremendous confidence among customers, bankers, vendors, and employees, and as such it is the greatest marketing message you will never pay for. As my mentor Alan Weiss says, "The first sale is always to yourself."

What happens, then, when an owner can't close the deal in his or her own mind? If a company flounders, ambivalence is the cause—but what causes ambivalence? Here are some common examples based on my experience with clients:

The Pain of Change is Greater than the Pain of Not Changing: There is no one more stoic than a business owner who accepts the pain of not growing as preferable to the risk of growing. Yes, fear is real and change can be drastic, but seizing the day is easier than it feels. So many times I have helped a business owner move out of his or her comfort zone. Even if it meant giving up on the business, it created conviction and allowed the owner to move on.

Perfectionism: One chronic example involves the inability to keep things simple. Many owners, particularly those with roots in corporate America or in possession of MBAs (no, I'm not picking on anybody; I got one too), strive to produce a "perfect plan." These people are used to the cloistered experience of corporations or academia, and they tend to analyze a problem forever. By tweaking every detail they end up delaying (or preventing) forward progress. This isn't procrastination, however, but perfectionism. Their greatest desire is to be perfect so that someone (the great business professor in the sky?) will bestow an A plus. Frequently, these owners believe that if they don't act they won't fail—until their business goes up in flames.

Groundhog Day: Some owners keep repeating past mistakes, but because they lack a wide-lens view of their actions, they aren't able to pinpoint the problems. These owners tend to be very frustrated. What could be more exhausting than running uphill at full speed and never making it to the top? They need to slow down. They need to take a good, long look at where they want to go and what they must do to get there. In most cases, these owners are terrific at what they do but know nothing about managing a business. They need a crash course in business school and often require an independent party, such as a consultant or advisor, to help them.

Denial: We all know the "if only" excuse, as in "If only I had better employees," or "better suppliers," or "better advertising." Everyone longs for things they don't have, whether it be a 32-inch waistline or a larger marketing budget. Too many business owners, however, see these desires as causes to fail instead of reasons to change. Successful people in all walks of life don't sit around wringing their hands over everything they lack. They are too busy turning what they've got into gold.

Fatalism: To believe that you have no control over your firm's destiny, markets, customers, employees, or vendors makes it hard to be active. Yet so many owners say "My business is different, it doesn't allow me to be decisive." I challenge anyone to pick any industry and I can find a company that is growing successfully by breaking the rules. In my hometown a famous restaurant just closed, blaming its misfortune on local businesses sponsoring fewer luncheons. Living in America's fattest city says otherwise. People are eating more than ever, just not in a traditional way that settled restaurants could count on. Unless you are selling leaded gas and the government bans your product, your target market has moved, not quit buying.

Ambivalence: The dark side

Ambivalence can strike at any time and take many forms. Sometimes it shows up as doubt, fear, and cautiousness, as owners who vacillate about which direction is least likely to wreck their companies end up missing their best opportunities. Other times, ambivalence masks itself as contentment. Owners who settle too comfortably into the status quo lack the determination to push themselves off the couch and on to the next level of growth. Whatever the situation, your business is at risk *if you are ambivalent.* In other words, if your business isn't growing as rapidly as you wish, you need to ask yourself why.

On those days when nothing goes right, when clients question your prices or value, employees complain more than they work, and machines from the copier to the conveyor belt to the coffee maker keep breaking down, what will keep you going? Owners who are afflicted with ambivalence and its fraternal twin, insecurity, have little defense against short- or long-term complications, frustrations, and daily distractions. Even when they know they must take corrective action, they have no foundation to make a decision. They are modern-day Hamlets, fretting and dithering until even a patient audience wants to yell, "Just *do* something!"

The steel in your spine

All business owners have a personal version of "the shot heard round the world"—the single event, moment, or culmination of experiences that led them to major change. I call this source of conviction a defining point, because it is the axis on which a person's attitude and actions rotate. For start-up entrepreneurs, this typically occurs when they decide they will never, ever work for someone else again! For experienced owners, the epiphany occurs (and reoccurs) when major challenges or opportunities force them out of their status quo. This is the moment of commitment to a new path.

We all know a defining point when we see it, although the details vary. Famous (or infamous) examples include these from reality and fiction:

- In the fifth game of the 1986 World Series, Red Sox first baseman Bill Buckner flubs the game's final grounder, igniting a Mets comeback that not only wins the game but ultimately the series. Sports announcers opine about "momentum," but this is a defining point. In one moment of carelessness, Buckner kindled the Mets' belief in themselves and satisfied the Red Sox's *conviction* that their team was cursed.

- In a film shown at the Rock and Roll Hall of Fame in Cleveland, the luminous Janis Joplin explains her famous statement "Freedom's just another word for nothing left to lose" as a result of her misfit childhood. Her peers may have "laughed her out of class, out of town, and out of the state," but from this rejection she launched her rebel self into becoming the greatest rock and blues singer of her generation.

- In the epic play *Les Misérables*, the hero, Jean Valjean, confesses to his pursuer (the Inspector) and then saves his life. This selfless gesture lifts Valjean from his fate, but drives his captor to question his purpose and ultimately, to commit suicide.

- In *Animal House*, Bluto Blutarski (an unlikely leader) rallies his frat house from ignominious defeat to a victorious destruction of the Faber College parade with this immortal battle cry: "We didn't quit when the Germans bombed Pearl Harbor!"

As these examples show, a defining point can be deadly serious and carry grave consequences, or it can be small and embarrassing, as when a corporate manager is turned away from a country club because his boss "forgot" to tell him that his membership had been cut off. A defining point also can be something positive, as in a mother's overwhelming love for her newborn that leads her to make a major life decision. It can be a process or a flash in time, such as that last Dilbert comic that struck too close to home and caused you to quit your job. Whatever the details, your defining point indicates the birth of your conviction. And it can guide you through making decisions about your daily activities, taking you ever closer to your goals.

Birol's bit: Yes, he gets my respect!

Rodney Dangerfield is the greatest movie entrepreneur of all time.

Yes, you read that right. The late, great Rodney, getter of no respect, exemplifies in life and on film the Everyman heart of a business owner. One of my favorite movies is *Back to School*, which should be on the DVD shelf of every business owner because of its celebration of entrepreneurial values.

Even if you've never seen it, you know the character Dangerfield plays—the guy who "gets no respect" partly because of his boorish behavior, but mostly because he gleefully exposes hypocrisy. The movie is an updated version of the children's story about the emperor who has no clothes; here the emperor is the puffed-up world of academia, and Dangerfield is the fifty-something "boy" who joins his son at college and becomes the voice of reason.

In *Back to School*, Rodney Dangerfield plays a tailor *par excellence*, an entrepreneur who has built a clothing empire and an entire worldview with a needle

Birol's bit: (continued)

and thread. His single-minded passion for men's clothing suggests the focus a successful business owner must possess; attending a literature class taught by Sally Kellerman, he "analyzes" Hemingway in terms of his being a great Big and Tall client for his store. Confident in the value of his own real-world experience, he explodes the microeconomics professor's theory of the firm as "being managed in fantasy land," then dismisses a report by the Rand Institute as being "too light" to earn a high grade. Weighing the report in his hand, he notes, "It feels like a B."

This is the same Dangerfield character we see in *Caddyshack*, a film in which he offends the establishment by besting its members, building condos within sight of the snobby country club, and proving wrong Ted Knight's assertion that "some people just don't belong." A classic American story: the triumph of the common man. Rodney Dangerfield enacts the entrepreneurial conviction that honesty, straightforwardness, humor, and excellence will trump corporate pedigrees, fancy MBAs, and PowerPoint presentations, every time.

I began my career as one of those corporate-MBA-PowerPoint guys, and the suit fit me like a hair shirt. It wasn't until I started embracing plain talk over pedigree that my own business really took off. This is a vital lesson for business owners who must rely on wits, experience, and personal drive to seize each opportunity to grow their company.

Clarifying your defining point

Remember Popeye the Sailor Man (and original Zen master) standing up to Bluto, spluttering, "That's all I can takes, 'cause I can't takes no more"? *That's* what a defining point feels like.

As a business owner, you are probably highly self-motivated, but do you know what got you started or keeps you going? Was it a flash realization or a series of events? What led to your decision to grow your own business, overcome obstacles, and ultimately succeed? To narrow down your defining point, answer these questions:

- When did your defining point occur?
- How did you know what your defining point was?
- Since your defining point occurred, what do you now know and do on a regular or semi-regular basis?
- Since your defining point occurred, what do you no longer believe or do on a regular or semi-regular basis?
- How does your defining point give you confidence?

Identifying this source of conviction is the first step toward growing your business because it will power your commitment to implement the knowledge, behaviors, and tools of successful owners. It will also help you reconcile your business, family, health, and other life challenges in a way that works for you. How can it accomplish so much?

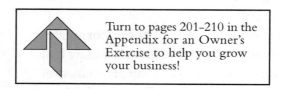

Turn to pages 201–210 in the Appendix for an Owner's Exercise to help you grow your business!

Perhaps the story of my own defining point will be instructive. At the time, I was the vice president of sales and marketing at a prosperous company. I had a big staff and an office to-die-for, with lots of gleaming glass and a

magnificent view. I made a great salary, yet I wasn't happy. .
chance to help define the company's direction and my boss wasn't givı..ָ
to me. One of the important lessons my corporate experience taught me is
that too many people try to achieve success based on what a company has
done in the past rather than on what it is capable of doing in the future. The
result is that they limit the growth of their organization. This is what I saw
happening.

At the same time my business life was proving unsatisfying, my family
was in crisis. My newborn daughter, Margo, had been diagnosed with
cystic fibrosis, an incurable and—at the time of this writing—fatal disease.
Cystic fibrosis devastates the respiratory and digestive systems of a child,
and Margo was in and out of the hospital. As I felt the pieces of my life
crumbling, my best friend from the office invited my wife and me to his
home for dinner one night, and he urged me to hang tough. He, too, was
frustrated in his job, but we promised to get through things together.

A week later, this same friend called me into his office. My boss had
him fire me. I gathered my coat and my last slip of pride and walked out.
Halfway to my car, my cell phone rang. It was my wife. Our daughter was
in the hospital with a severe infection in her lungs.

Rushing to the hospital, I thought about my family, mortgage, medical
bills, and responsibilities. I felt like a victim of my own circumstances,
powerless, with no safety net. When I got to the hospital my little girl was
hooked up to tubes and monitors that did nothing to diminish the fire in
her eyes. And in that instant, I knew she was going to live. Margo was
simply doing what she did best, fighting for her life. In that moment, I
knew I owed it to her to fight for mine.

The next day, I started my consulting practice. It has brought me
prosperity and, more importantly, tremendous satisfaction *because I am
doing what I ought to be doing.* My daily tasks are aligned with my passions
(to help owners grow their companies), my talents (assessing challenges
and opportunities and helping companies implement solutions), and even
my character flaws (impatience, bossiness, and a take-no-prisoners way of
speaking—all positive tools for consultants)!

So many times in our lives, it takes a crisis to set us on the path we should have been on all along. My defining point was harsh, but it had to be loud for me to get the point. I hope yours doesn't have to be so cruel. If you ask yourself the tough questions every day, perhaps your defining moments can be more like visits from old friends and less like axes falling on your head!

Greed or ego: Pick your poison

Once you determine your defining point, it's time to consider the force behind it. Anyone who is serious about running a business has a need to succeed beyond the common wish for a contented, uncomplicated life. Although many factors come into play, the two most common motives behind this kind of ambition are ego and greed.

In my experience, and against the teachings of most churches and holistic schools of thought, owners motivated by greed are the ones most likely to grow their business. Why? The ego-driven owner is more likely to make decisions that are not based on the firm's ability to resolve customer pain or create opportunities because he or she is focused on stature, trappings, and history or reputation. He or she often waits too long to make hard decisions that place him or her in an unflattering light, such as shutting down an initiative, terminating a family member, or moving to an austerity or zero-based budget.

This type of owner is too proud to understand that the marketplace has changed and the cost structure, production facilities, employees' expertise, and abilities have fallen out of grace with what customers and prospects are buying *now*. Ironically, this owner is also more likely to carve out a legacy as a philanthropist, sometimes sacrificing funds that could be used to strengthen the company.

In contrast, the greed driven owner is focused on the bottom line. When it's all about making money, the owner is more likely to take quick, necessary actions to keep the company prosperous. Earning more means selling more, which means serving customers in more and better ways. By putting profit above prestige, this owner is objective about pursuing customer needs and often creates a legacy surpassing that of the ego-driven owner.

Anyone who has flown in an airplane knows the rule of self-preservation: put on your own oxygen mask before helping with anyone else's. A company that is drowning in its owner's unquenchable desire for control or need for recognition won't have the strength to survive. Greed translates into the confidence to make smart decisions in the best interest of the company, whether it means pricing for value or making objective decisions regarding family members or friends who work for the firm. The higher the profits, the more generous and active the role a company can take toward the owner's favorite causes—and the more confidently an owner can draw the line if a family member's behavior comes at the expense of the company, customers, or employees.

If you build it

Yet another dimension of an owner's correct mindset involves striking the right balance between pragmatism and blind faith. Think of all those dot-com flameouts: just because you build it doesn't mean any customers will come.

Very large companies may have the resources to be everything to their customers, but small and mid-sized businesses risk diluting their excellence—the reason they attracted their customers in the first place—by trying to do too much at one time. They also risk the company's health, because unless a firm has a large cash reserve to pour into a new venture, it may run out of money before the "investment" pays for itself.

As you will see in Chapter 2, the one-stop shopping approach is antithetical to my philosophy of Best and Highest Use, which requires owners to make their firms special to a select group of customers who will appreciate and pay for this brand of excellence. How many times have you been pursued by sales reps offering you way too many solutions to a small, specific problem? All you want is a long distance line, but the phone company keeps haranguing you about DSL, cell phone packages, voice mail, and caller ID. This isn't meeting customer needs, it's running them down with a bulldozer.

Customers have specific needs, and many feel resentful toward aggressive sales people who talk to their money instead of their faces. Rather than throwing the kitchen sink at them, build loyalty by taking the time to understand what customers need *from their perspective.* How would you feel if someone assumed he or she knew more about your business and its needs than you do?

On the other hand, you do want to maximize profits, so adding value in the form of products and services that are related to your company's BHU is a great idea. The key is to strike a balance to satisfy your desire to sell and your customers' desire to purchase. If forced to buy a total solutions package, customers are likely to defect at the first sign of disappointment, especially when the relationship is new. They would rather try out your company's ability to deliver on its promises before making a major commitment.

For example, when I served as Product Manager for the Bank of Boston, we built customer loyalty using a toe-in-the-water approach. We started by offering CD's with competitive rates to attract prospects who wanted their money in a safe place. We then developed a rollover program to encourage investors to stay with us, banking on the idea that the longer they held the CDs, the more likely they were to open a checking account. By studying your customers' typical buying behavior, you will be able to design valuable products and services to meet their needs, and offer them in an order that will benefit customers when they need it. This isn't "total solutions" selling—it's just smart business.

Passion can be mistaken for blind faith, and blind faith has killed many businesses. (Okay, it's built some really good ones, too, but let's go with the odds.) Astute owners balance the faith of knowing they can implement, sell, and deliver new ideas with the pragmatic necessity to make money doing so. Don't leap into any new venture before taking a hard-eyed look at what you can sacrifice in terms of cash, time, people, and other resources. Otherwise, that "conviction" is really just wishful thinking.

Looks like you've made it

One of the most enjoyable aspects of my business is watching others make the steep transition to entrepreneurship. After years of seeing venture capitalists and other financial gamers flail about in the ocean of ownership, I am convinced that few financial intermediaries make great owners. They generally aren't passionate about what they sell. They talk in terms of roll ups, cash outs, and other financial gimmicks instead of focusing on delighting their customers, living their products and services, and standing behind all that they sell. Likewise, corporate players who try to cut and paste corporate tactics into a new business won't experience the freedom— or the success—that comes with building a company brick-by-brick on the strength of the owner's distinctiveness.

Whatever their background, the winners are those who discard the trappings, the ego, and the support mechanisms and develop and understanding of what owning a business is all about—delivering customer value. Here's an example: A client of mine, Paul Cervelloni, had talent coming out of his eyeballs and an impressive résumé, including a stint as Chief Information Officer for a very large company. When it filed Chapter 11, however, Paul found himself pounding the pavement for a new job— until he realized he didn't want one! Suddenly, unemployment seemed like an opportunity to reinvent himself. He didn't like working for big companies. He was an entrepreneur at heart.

Paul's conviction was apparent in his decision to enroll in a sales training program. He had never sold anything in his life but knew he would need the skills as an independent IT consultant. He later described this training as "one of the best things" he'd ever done for his career. Before long, he had lined up a few contracts and his firm, CSI, was born.

Over the next four years, Paul provided a range of high-level IT services for one client after another, taking pretty much any business that came his way. "I was much happier," he said, "but I wasn't meeting my financial goals. There always seemed to be a lag, where I would do very well for a few months, but when that contract ended and the client was happy with what I had done, I was out of work again."

Paul had built his business up from nothing on the strength of his conviction, but he needed to reinforce it. Soon after he hired me, I insisted he focus on doing one thing and doing it really well. Similar to a lot of skittish owners, he was afraid specializing would make him less marketable, but exactly the opposite was true. By hiring himself out to so many companies, from small businesses to big corporations, and selling so many different products and services, he had not created an identity for his business. (And the name CSI didn't help. The TV show, which debuted after Paul started using the name, was already a ratings king.) Paul was proficient at many things, but together we pinpointed his highest value in serving large sourcing IT or big process outsourcing, which let him work with both buyers and sellers to negotiate fair deals. He was uniquely positioned to serve both sides of a huge untapped market: buyers and sellers who needed each other and who would benefit from a "win-win" approach based on fairness, transparency, and clear expectations.

The result? Having changed the name of his firm to Cervelloni Services, Inc. (and not stressing the acronym), Paul is growing his business at a brisk pace. He continues to exceed his financial goals. And he is more enthusiastic than ever, building his business on the unique value he offers to customers.

Similar to Paul Cervelloni, many talented, motivated achievers have a high threshold for pain, to the point that professional setbacks may fuel their determination to succeed in jobs they don't really enjoy. Decide where your conviction lies. To run your own firm, you must be willing and eager to accept more responsibility, authority, and risk in performing activities you truly enjoy. This blend of passion, skills, and joy creates the perfect entrepreneurial fuel. Draw on your conviction to power your efforts to find, keep, and grow customers and take your business to the next level.

Success in our time

I want to close this chapter with a quick look at some of the great achievers I know. Here are a few owners who discarded their ambivalence and accelerated the growth of their firms:

- By focusing on a single target with tremendous confidence and conviction, John Bukovnik has transformed Easy2 Software into an Internet powerhouse. The company didn't exist 10 years ago. Today it is an exclusive provider to the home improvement giant Lowe's and to many of the Lowe's vendors, making Easy2 a leader in the industry.

- Under the leadership of Howard Garfinkle, Superior Tool keeps inventing and manufacturing new plumbing tools for the building trades. The company's ability to pioneer products for the most mature of markets is testament to Garfinkle's commitment to the "basics." This is a primary ingredient of Garfinkle's BHU and is a cornerstone for the his business success.

- The demand for security products and services is expanding, and no one is better poised to serve this market than Integrated Precision Systems. Led by Jim Butkovic, IPS supplies building access and employee identification solutions to the nation's largest shopping malls and other clients. Jim's dedication to customer service lifts his company above the crowd and serves as a standard for any owner who wants to work both smart and hard.

- Wittco Standard, a family-owned supplier of office and graphic arts equipment, found itself competing with the rest of the world when anonymous Internet discounters invaded their industry. President John Massie led the company's efforts to reinvent itself. By prioritizing terrific customer service, Massie and his team developed a tier of product-service combinations to appeal to a range of customers and boost profits through high-end packages.

Are these guys lucky? Do they possess some kind of Midas touch that turns their decisions into profits? Absolutely not. The "magic" they possess is the self-confidence that arises from believing in their companies. Their triumphs are the living, breathing examples of my own core conviction: that as business owners, we each control our own destiny through the passion and conviction we either *do* or *don't* possess.

☑ Self-check: Ambivalence

Ambivalence is to the business owner what salty food is to an obese smoker with high blood pressure—a silent killer. Check the following symptoms to find out whether you are ambivalent. Do you agree with any of the following statements?

☐ My products or services aren't all that effective.

☐ My customers don't really deserve the best.

☐ My employees are replaceable.

☐ Sure, I can cut corners. Who'll notice?

☐ What, me lead? Leadership doesn't really matter.

A "yes" answer to one or more of these statements indicates some level of ambivalence.

Chapter 2

The Conviction-to-Customer Connection: Developing your Best and Highest Use

It is the late 1980s. I am driving on Martha's Vineyard, sun glinting off the ocean, breeze rippling through my (then full head of) hair, and listening to the radio when James Taylor comes on the air. A local resident, he has been asked to play a few of his hits and take questions from listeners.

"Oh, *James*," gushes a female voice. I turn down my radio volume. "You sing so *well!* You have such a beautiful *voice!* I just *love* to listen to you!"

"Why, thank you," says Taylor, after a beat. "That's important in my line of work."

Almost 20 years later, his words still make me laugh. James Taylor exemplifies the purpose-driven entrepreneur. His singing voice is easy on the ears, sure, but he knows it alone doesn't make him distinct. *American Idol* has proven that a lot of people can carry a tune (and even more people can't). What makes James Taylor a star? He writes his own songs, and he knows exactly what type of songs his audience wants him to sing.

While he lacks the range and soulfulness of Van Morrison and the versatility of Paul Simon, other stars of his era, Taylor has a genius for introspection, nostalgia, and wordplay, all delivered through the warm comfort of his voice. Thirty years after hitting the national scene, he still writes, records, and tours, thus reinforcing his base of support. He loves his work, does it well, and delivers a product that delights his customers. James Taylor has found his Best and Highest Use.

Conviction made manifest

What do you love to do? What does your firm do well? Why does anyone buy your products and services? Many owners find it difficult to answer these questions because many businesses do not have a clear reason for being. These firms subsist rather than succeed, flowing along with one new trend after another until they get caught in a whirlpool.

Without a sense of purpose, owners pursue survival and sales objectives as if these tactics will lead to wealth, long life, and happiness. In contrast, the stars within any marketplace—a James Taylor, Michael Dell, or Bill Gates, for example—clearly understand their own core competencies and prosper from them. Since Joseph Campbell coined the phrase "follow your bliss" many years ago, writers, therapists, and high school guidance counselors have been urging people to make their dreams come true. There's nothing wrong with this, except nobody bothers to explain how to do it. So, let's get practical. Conviction, the crucial first catalyst, means nothing unless you translate it into the reality of the marketplace by connecting your passion to the needs of your customers.

In its purest form, Best and Highest Use (BHU) is the point of convergence between what you *love to do* and *do well* and what *customers want or need* and *will pay to get*. Don't confuse BHU with the actual products or services you sell. Rather, it is the purpose *behind* the products and services you sell, so it remains a reservoir of energy and ideas that connect you with your customers' changing needs. Best and Highest Use manifests your preferences and talents in ways that fill needs in the marketplace:

- *Your Best* represents your preferred choice of profession amongst all the things you do well.
- *Highest* represents your value that is most valued by customers, suppliers, employers, or partners.

- *Use* is the actual, essential value you provide to your customers, clients, employees, and others.

Unless you have all three elements, you and your company will eventually experience boredom, dissatisfaction, mediocrity, chaos, or feeble sales and frail profits. Best and Highest Use begins in passion (the owner's), is refined through need (the customer's), and ends in satisfaction all around. When the marketplace says, "Yes, *that* is what you should be doing to give me what I need!" you have found your BHU.

One of the first things I do with new clients is to take them through the process of identifying their BHU, so get a notebook and a pen. Work through the following sections for now, and don't forget to complete the exercises for this chapter (located in the appendix).

Turn to pages 210–215 in the Appendix for an Owner's Exercise to help you grow your business!

Document your successes

List all the things you do well, both practical and impractical. Brainstorm; set a timer for 10 minutes and jot down everything that comes to mind, even if it has nothing to do with business. Examine your list several times over the next few days, looking for skills and talents (both sung and unsung).

Your personal strengths are the power behind the value you offer to customers. For example, a licensed realtor starting her own company once led her college debate team to a state championship but nearly flunked statistics. She is a crack negotiator, and this strength is the foundation for her firm.

If you are a sole-proprietor or have only a few employees, your personal talents will drive your firm; otherwise, make a separate list of things your company does well. These may be mundane or dramatic. Remember the 1982 Tylenol crisis, when seven people died after someone laced several bottles of pills with cyanide? Johnson & Johnson set the standard for crisis management by recalling $100 million worth of product and introducing tamper-resistant caplets in triple-sealed packages. Several years later, during a similar though less deadly tampering scare, Tylenol marketed itself as the company to trust, and consumers believed it.

Consider the importance of fun

List the tasks, relationships, and experiences you enjoy, both now and in the past. Look for examples in your personal and professional lives. Whatever you think of the National Rifle Association, Charlton Heston relished his role as NRA president. My former employer, New England Business Service, takes pride in replacing the business forms customers lose in natural disasters. This enjoyment drives future success, confidence, and self-esteem.

Discover what clients, customers, and staff like about you

Hire a trusted third-party to talk to your customers and employees. You will get some remarkable feedback. One of my clients, Inside Prospects, boasts the best list of businesses in Cleveland, but what customers most value is the personal service provided by its president, Sandy Szuch. This is an element of her business she can't afford to lose.

Distill and simplify

Turn your strengths into your message. For example, based on its reputation, resources, and breadth of businesses, General Electric rightly claimed to "Bring good things to life." Warren Buffett, the world's greatest investor, is known for having said, "If I don't understand it, I don't invest in it."

Know your blind spots

Too many organizations are proud of themselves in ways that don't matter. How many customers really care if a business is family-owned or has a 100-year history? Some companies waste millions promoting features and services that are irrelevant to their customers.

Synthesize, apply, and focus

Work with an objective outsider to put it all together. Take the combination of skills, experience, and expertise and state it in terms of what a customer, prospect, or marketplace wants. For example, Ralph Lauren has leveraged his ability to define grace in everyday living not only through a classic clothing line but across a home products empire as well. And no matter how much Microsoft wants to be known as an innovator, Bill Gates' obvious genius is to exploit other developers' inventions into necessary tools for all computer users.

Apply these steps and you will gain new insight into your business and its customers. And customers will notice. The relentless logic of the marketplace demands that you deliver solid value to customers in order to keep them loyal to your business, and as they respond positively, your comfort zone will expand.

Client case study: Felber & Felber Marketing

Best and Highest Use is the great equalizer for small companies trying to compete with large, well-resourced firms. I have worked with scores of owners who face this challenge, including Rob and Bruce Felber, brothers and partners in their own marketing firm. The Felbers provided exceptional service and delighted their customers, but they had innovated their way out of a stable income stream. After founding their business in 1993, then called Traymore Marketing, the brothers developed "three-dimensional marketing" to cut through the clutter of direct mail. One successful campaign was designed for a national fiber-optic Internet provider promoting the speed of its new service. The Felbers developed a remote-control racecar, complete with batteries, but mailed the packages without the remote control. To get their car to work, people had to visit the ISP's Website or call a company representative—and people wanted those cars to work!

A 1 percent response rate is typical for conventional direct mailings, but the Felbers were delivering rates as high as 10 to 20 percent for their clients. The problem for the firm was the high level of customization required for each dimensional package. Traditional advertising agencies rely on steady revenues, which Rob and Bruce couldn't get from specialized campaigns, so they spread themselves thin, selling off their talents in pieces to anyone who would pay. It was like selling chewing gum, one stick at a time.

More than a decade into the life of their firm, the Felbers still had trouble winning clients away from big-name firms, even though they offered full-service capabilities. As Rob said, "Too many customers didn't care." The reason? Beyond the cool customized campaigns the brothers designed, clients didn't understand what the firm was about. Dimensional marketing was a product, not a purpose, and it was something big companies could duplicate. Rob and Bruce needed to define their BHU, and we found it in their ability and passion for teaching.

Most ad agencies keep clients dependent so profits keep rolling in, but what about companies that don't want or can't afford to outsource all their marketing? These customers were out there, and nobody was serving them. What an opportunity for two guys with natural teaching skills! Together we redefined their firm—and renamed it Felber & Felber Marketing—as a unique communications shop offering full-service marketing capabilities and/or customized training to clients seeking to do their own campaigns.

Rob explained it this way: "Once we are in the client's door, we give them a choice. We come in and analyze resources, develop models, and execute models to tweak performance. At that point, we can continue to execute, or give the model back to the client with training on how to use it." This option clearly separates Felber & Felber from bigger agencies. Contrast this with the old method of selling gum. "We weren't giving people a clear picture of who we were," Rob said, "because we weren't clear about who we wanted to be." Best and Highest Use focused the brothers, giving them, in the words of Bruce Felber, "a niche and position in the marketplace and clarity about the future."

Reaping the benefits of BHU

Many years ago, my friend Fred Bacon said, "You know, Andy, people act in their own self interest. And don't try to change them." I argued that if a mother has only enough food to feed herself or her hungry baby, she'll feed the baby first. "Exactly my point!" he said. "The mother would rather be hungry than deal with her grief of seeing her baby starve. It's in her self-interest!" A key benefit of Best and Highest Use is its ability to unite everyone's self-interest (the owner's ego and the employees' efforts) with what is best for the company and for the customer. How does this work? Let's consider some of the advantages of operating from BHU.

Owner's confidence

Some days you face so many decisions, both trivial and critical, that you may long for a Magic 8–Ball to tell you what to do. A less random (and more accurate) tool, BHU simplifies the hundreds of problems you face down to a few that really matter. Without all the clutter, you can interpret the problems rather than focus on symptoms. Best and Highest Use provides a common lens and a guiding philosophy for your actions and results, letting you slice through competing agendas to get to what matters and implement solutions. Imagine a 15–year old girl shaking that Magic 8–Ball and asking, "But does he like me? Does he really like me?" Gazing into the purple murk of her future, she sees this message float to the top: *Go study for your math test.* That's the power of BHU!

Employee conviction and performance

You've probably heard the old saying, "It is better to be lucky than smart." Well, why not be both? Do you want to trust your fate to something as random as luck?

I have already shared the story of being fired from a corporate vice-presidency on the same day my child was in the hospital fighting for her life. My business was born out of an unshakeable conviction that no one would ever possess that much control over my life again. But the story doesn't start there. My defining point was a culmination of observations, aggravations, and rude awakenings experienced throughout my career.

I was an "atypical" American boy, brought up in New York but transplanted to Turkey at age six. I returned at age 12 and fell head-over-heels for the American entrepreneurial dream. The thrill of succeeding as a paperboy and raffle ticket salesman instilled in me the exhilarating power of self-sufficiency. It wasn't until I began working for large corporations that I faced company politics. To make a long story short, I was up-sized, down-sized, right-sized, and ended up super-sized. Along the way, different managers in different companies appraised me, using the same criteria, as being at the top and the bottom of the same scales. How could this be? And it wasn't just happening to me. I watched countless star performers stumble while others, despite dismal efforts or mediocre abilities, rose to higher levels.

This made no sense. I had been brought up to believe that the resources of leadership, money, time, and expertise, if properly executed, would create the results of consistently successful companies. Why wasn't this happening? What explained the disconnection between the means of excellence and the ends of success—or the means of mediocrity and the ends of promotion?

Reflecting upon the talents of the employees and leaders around me, I located two sources. First, employees are motivated by the desire to cover their own tails. Circumventing the boss, whether to pursue innovation or correct the boss's errors, is a good way to get fired, so most employees go along to get along. This type of culture guarantees mediocrity by devaluing creativity and risk. Annual reviews that bear little connection to marketplace results, the handcuffs of long-term benefits programs, and a stultifying political correctness together create a culture of self-interest masked by a devotion to propriety, hierarchy, and groupthink.

Second, those winners at the top of the corporate hierarchy exhibit self-interest on steroids, prioritizing their own financial well-being and reputation over the company's long-term stability and growth. The "system" rewards corporate leaders for playing games, including financial short-cutting, divorcing their own compensation from company performance, and in general, resisting change, avoiding commitments, and sandbagging their responsibilities to grow the company.

My faith that success would follow from goodness was broken, and I figured that if big companies couldn't put their vast resources to good use, what chance did a rough and tumble, under-resourced venture have? Astonishingly, however, the small business owners around me were enjoying more success than their larger counterparts. The reason was Best and Highest Use, which unites the individual self-interest of company, owner, and employees to build wealth all around.

In so doing, BHU explains what otherwise might be seen as plain dumb luck. Whereas the traditional corporate culture levels individual differences down to the lowest common denominator, BHU celebrates uniqueness, matching skills and passion within the context of a firm's environment. As individuals, we gravitate toward things we like to do and are good at, and toward people who share our passions. Often this movement is unconscious, as when you discover that the stranger you chatted up at last week's luncheon grew up two blocks from your childhood home. When owners shape their companies around BHU, they distinguish themselves from other firms. This is critical for entrepreneurs, whose energy, drive, and creativity attract people with the same qualities. Innovation, individuality, and passion become company values.

Best and Highest Use involves redefining the best way to serve your market, create value, and use your company's resources, all of which effect the fate of your employees. By giving your staff a personal stake in the company's fortunes, you encourage loyalty.

Happy customers, happy company

By determining what makes your firm truly special, you will be able to target your *best* prospects and customers—those most likely to respond to your offer—and design sales, marketing, and customer service efforts that speak to them. This requires you to know as much as you can about your prospects and customers, and as you deepen your understanding of the way they use your products and services, you will discover new and profitable opportunities for serving them. By driving your BHU throughout your company, you can cut costs, boost profits, and develop a brand, all the while finding, keeping, and growing more customers.

The PACER Process

Many years ago I created a system to help owners identify, articulate, and apply their Best and Highest Use. The PACER Process is a Process for Acquiring Customers and Enhancing Retention. It is particularly suited for owner-driven companies because those of us possessing the classic entrepreneurial personality need a system to stay on track. Our tendency to take on too many responsibilities and tasks, including ones outside our area of mastery, sets us up to become distracted, exhausted, tolerant of mediocrity, overly critical of self and others, obsessed with details or neglectful of details, and all-around burned out. The PACER Process keeps owners focused on what matters. The next chapter explains the sales funnels portion of the PACER Process, so for now we will lay a foundation. Guess what? It's called BHU.

Step 1: Clarify your Best and Highest Use

Quickly answer the following questions for you and your business:
- What do you love to do?
- What do you do really well?
- What do your customers like about your business?
- Which specific problems does your business resolve for your customers?

If you were in college, this would be a pop quiz—a check to see whether you worked through the steps to identify your BHU. Did you pass? If not, go back a few pages and complete the steps.

You will refine your BHU as you discover more about your strengths, your firm's abilities, and your customers' needs, but you need a place to begin. Be honest and specific. The more explicit your BHU, the more tangible your efforts to connect with customers.

Step 2: Identify your target market

Your target market is the pool of prospects with the potential to become your best customers. In other words, these are the people whose needs are most closely aligned with what you offer.

Best and Highest Use immunizes companies against the "Be All Things to All People" disease, one that is as common as a cold but deadly as the plague. Is your business afflicted? What happens if you don't target a specific market?

- Your company isn't special; it is mediocre, forgettable, or worse.
- People can't refer customers to you.
- You attract unqualified prospects.
- You waste resources on prospects who don't care about your offer, therefore diminishing your efforts towards prospects who do.

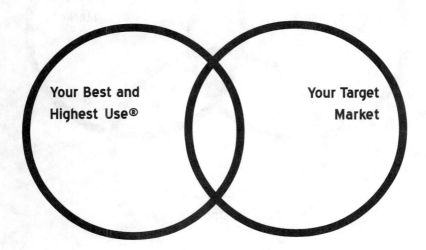

Some owners, particularly of small companies or start-ups, fret about losing sales by making their target too small. But which group deserves the bulk of your marketing resources—the 500 companies within your broad market, of which you close 10 percent, or the 100 companies within your target market, of which you close 50 percent? Yes, math brains, you have closed 50 customers in each example. But imagine how much higher you margins are when you don't have to market to those extra 400 prospects? Not to mention the retention rate. Whether you are a retailer, distributor, manufacturer, or service provider, delivering your BHU to a narrow group of satisfied customers is the fastest way to create loyal customers. You excel, they exult, and they keep coming back!

So, who are your best customers? Why do they buy from you? Can you identify them beyond common markers such as SIC code, sales volume, and number of employees? Targeting a market means understanding the customers' perception of what they are buying from you. This may not be what you think you are selling.

Step 3: The crucial intersection

Your company's *best use* will resolve the *greatest pain* or creates the *greatest opportunity* for a *narrow slice* of your market. This is the *crucial intersection* between your Best and Highest Use and the needs of your customers.

The prospects and customers located in this sweet spot place the highest value on what you have to offer. Treat them right, and they are most likely, among all prospects in your market, to become loyal, long-term customers and advocates of your business. Don't they deserve the bulk of your marketing, sales, and customer service activities?

Of the three circles in the PACER Process, two are customer-focused: one describes the customer; the other describes the customer's pain or opportunity. Features and benefits are fine, but customers purchase outcomes. Let's use Rob and Bruce Felber as examples. A large company over-spending (in money, time, and headaches) on a mediocre in-house marketing department is in pain. To resolve that pain, Felber & Felber Marketing could provide comprehensive advertising for less (in money, time, and headaches) than the company was paying employees. On the other hand, a sole-proprietor with limited resources but a creative mind wants to start building a brand and expand locally; Felber & Felber could help him seize this opportunity by delivering a model and training him to run his own marketing in the future.

While much has been written about experience marketing, solution selling, and consultative selling, the truth is simpler. Customers want to know how you can help them be successful, avoid risk, and seize opportunity. They want you to understand their business and their fears, hopes, objectives, and dreams.

What a buyer wants

Fans of the *Pink Panther* movies may recall the scene in which Inspector Clousseau asks a young lady walking a dog, "Does your dog bite?" She says no, so he reaches down to pet the pooch and gets chomped. "I thought your dog doesn't bite," he yells. "Yes," she replies, "but that's not my dog."

Companies don't buy. The people within them do, and their position with the company determines their motivation, expectations, and authority. To sell, you must know whether the person sitting across the table is an employee, an executive, or an owner. Employees, operating out of a desire to meet their boss's objectives, do not have the authority to reach beyond their assignment. When IBM assured us that "no one ever got fired for picking IBM," they were talking to that employee in fear of the ultimate reprisal. Here are some tips for appealing to employee buyers:

- Offer tactical solutions to meet a single objective.
- Forget total solutions or one-stop shopping.
- Offer strong guarantees that meet the buyer's goal of staying out of trouble.
- Create standards to measure your performance against their objective. They can use these standards as much to protect themselves as to hold you accountable.
- Promise them opportunities for recourse and other options to protect their own positions inside their corporation.

Here is what to know when selling your products to corporate leaders:

- Sell strategic solutions that let them achieve their company's visions.
- Sell peer-to-peer. They have enough subordinates and sycophants.
- Create heft and credibility during the selling process.
- Build deep, multiple relationships throughout their organization.

Selling owner-to-owner might seem easy, but only if you know which stage of growth the owner is in. Regardless of industry or size of company, all owners go through three predictable stages towards success: 1) fear of failure; 2) increasing wealth; and 3) creating a legacy. By targeting the appropriate motivation, you can match your offer to that need. Here are some tips:

- Sell owner-to-owner. Your common entrepreneurial bind is an asset.
- Sell to the person, not just the company. The two are indivisible.
- Appeal to their business needs, but understand egos and personalities.
- Display empathy as well as the ability to lead them to success.

What Best and Highest Use is not

I've had the privilege of learning, using, and teaching a variety of growth tools for organizations. We've used a variety of names for these processes: Strategic planning, management by objectives, sales management, and incentive compensation. Too often, these systems "steamroller" over the interests of the users. Old-fashioned autocratic tools just don't work anymore.

More than a few times I have had people challenge me on my concept of Best and Highest Use, saying it is just another term for distinctive competence, one of those buzzwords that make the rounds of corporations and MBA programs. In one way, they are right. Best and Highest Use is essentially distinctive competence for business owners. The difference, and it's a large one, is that while distinctive competence speaks clinically of skill sets and marketplace advantages, BHU involves the owner's emotions, goals, and personality.

One concept I hear kicked around is "best practices." An accountant I know always boasts of how his statistics are above the average of his best practices group. But doesn't this assume that all firms start out and grow and stay completely equal? To center your business on best practices is to deny, ignore, and disrespect your BHU. How can you ever tell if you are better or worse than you should be if you only judge yourself on the basis of the lowest common denominator of other firms?

When it comes to my own business, I consider my biggest competitor to be inertia. (As a prospect once asked, "Where is the Inertia Company headquartered?" I responded, "Right here, but there are other branches everywhere.") The only thing you need to know in detail about your competitors is how they are resolving pain or creating opportunity for their customers—who could become *your* customers if you figure out a better way to serve their needs. Otherwise, your competitors have almost nothing to do with your progress.

The entrepreneurial advantage

When a company defines its Best and Highest Use and stays true to the vision, everything else falls into place. Yet few organizations do this. Instead, valuable time, energy, and resources are consumed by an obsession with tactics. We fixate on market demand and living through the next crisis, and we may even call it success. It's an empty success, the difference between dog-paddling and doing the breaststroke. Hey, we're not drowning, so we must be swimming, right? Except that land is nowhere in sight.

The beauty of Best and Highest Use is that it combines the immediately practical with long-term visions of growth. It links individuals to the company and ultimately to capitalism. It creates partnerships with employees by creating a common goal and a message to communicate to the masses, whether they are employees, vendors, or current and potential customers.

When a company leader recognizes and nurtures BHU, everyone with a stake in the company's success can pull together to produce powerful results. The message is clear: As a business owner, it all starts with you!

Chapter 3

From First Dates to Diamond Anniversaries: Enhancing your sales funnel to find, keep, and grow customers

A sign once hung in the Boston University Health Clinic:

> Sex
> The Pleasure: Momentary.
> The Position: Ridiculous.
> The Effort: Unwarranted.

The last point is debatable depending on your objective. The sign promoted abstinence among college students—quite a marketing challenge—so it pertains to the potentially calamitous consequences of casual sex. It's hard to explain to a 19-year old, but the urge to merge is about procreation, not fun. From an evolutionary standpoint, *all* romantic relationships, whether they last a few days or 50 years, are social constructs protecting nature's basic imperative: survival of the species. After all, most relationships evolve according to pattern. First we try out potential mates through dating, eventually finding someone with whom we enter into a (more or less) permanent union, which usually consists of marriage. A great number of these permanent unions produce children. The families constructed during this process become the touchstones of our lives, helping us to endure hard times and to celebrate good ones.

Although many people try to separate the personal from the professional, sometimes it is easier to realize that business deals are simply relationships that involve money. Customers buy from the people in your company, and they keep buying as they develop strong and healthy relationships with those people. Think of it this way:

- Finding customers is similar to dating.
- Keeping customers is similar to marriage.
- Growing customers is similar to families raising children.

Here is the beauty of the analogy. These relationship milestones are all chronological, with the success of each step resting on the completion and success of the previous step. Without having a strong foundation in the previous stage of development, the enterprise will ultimately crumble. We can see why owners get in trouble, for example, by proposing marriage to a prospect before asking him or her to a movie, or by treating a long-time loyal customer with the polite disinterest of a bad date.

Building on the basics

To grow your business, you only need to do three things, but you need to do them very well. While we can all relate to the anxiety of an owner who runs around shrieking, "Sales! I need more sales!" a better mantra would be "Court more prospects, recommit to more buyers, and extend relationships with loyal customers." In other words:

- Find customers.
- Keep customers.
- Grow customers.

What about all those sales, marketing, and customer service solutions that gloss over this simple truth? When courted by suitors who are as expensive as they are seductive, heed this sage advice: *Just Say No.*

Protecting your assets

We business owners are a profligate group, and temptation is everywhere. Sales training seminars, marketing gurus, next generation computer systems, software that promises to reach out and touch our customers, and so much more. All the while, the truth is free and right in front of us. *Steady, profitable, satisfying growth is all about finding, keeping, and growing customers.*

Don't get me wrong. Many sales, marketing, and customer service solutions can produce terrific results, but they are tactics, not goals. They are the means to an end of finding, keeping, and growing customers. There is no magic formula to consummate our desire for business growth, only the day-to-day work of building relationships with prospects and customers.

The PACER Process keeps your eyes on the prize of attracting prospects and bonding with customers. Let's start with a quick review. In the previous chapter, we defined the crucial intersection as the sweet spot where your firm's best use resolves the greatest pain or creates the most opportunity for a narrow slice of your marketplace.

The more narrowly you define this intersection, the better you can pinpoint your prospects and channel your resources toward those who are most likely to benefit from your offer. State it in terms of the following:

- What you do or make.
- For whom you do it.
- How they use it.
- How people can purchase it.
- What they've gained once they've bought it.

Your description must reveal your confidence, conviction, and clear understanding of how your company's Best and Highest Use will provide a desirable outcome for your prospect. Now you are ready to use the PACER Process sales funnels.

PACER Process sales funnels

The funnels look like a simplified sales, marketing, and customer service systems, right? So are they tactics? No, and here's why. Picture an apple sectioned into four slices. Pick up the slices, fit them back together, and you still have an apple, right? The funnels work the same way. You simply take your goal of finding customers and slice it into categories to represent how far you have moved prospects toward your goal. The customer acquisition funnel is a goal organized, but it's still a goal.

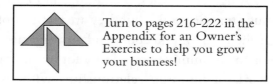

Turn to pages 216–222 in the Appendix for an Owner's Exercise to help you grow your business!

Acquisition Sales Funnel

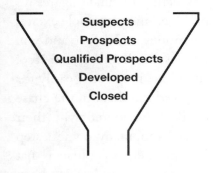

The *acquisition sales funnel* systematizes your activities to turn suspects into prospects, prospects into qualified prospects, and qualified prospects into buyers.

Retention Sales Funnel

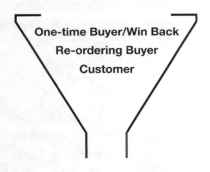

The *retention sales funnel* progressively moves one-time buyers (or ex-customers) to the desired status of customers who make multiple or sustained purchases.

Development Sales Funnel

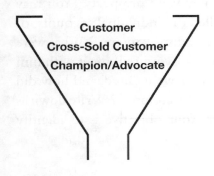

The *development sales funnel* moves stable customers through activities that convert them into up-sold/cross-sold customers and then to the status of advocate or champion.

Dating: The customer acquisition sales funnel

Prospecting begins with identifying your targets and ends with a signed contract or bill of sale. Some owners enjoy prospecting. Naturally aggressive and sociable, they relish the thrill of the hunt. Meeting new people excites them. They enjoy risking resources of time, money, and effort, and will do whatever it takes to get what they want. Does this describe you? If so, you are a natural hunter and the prospecting phase may come easily for you. I have known entrepreneurs who so enjoyed the thrill of the chase that they overemphasized prospecting and then wondered why their business kept losing customers. On the other hand, many owners step back from prospecting as soon as possible. The problem, of course, is that today's steady sales turn into next quarter's stagnant sales unless you keep signing new business. Whether you love the hunt or would rather play golf, the acquisition sales funnel can help you develop a predictable, duplicable process for finding customers without sacrificing profitability. The next few sections will help you to customize an acquisition sales funnel for your firm.

Look for patterns of behavior

Human behavior is eminently predictable. Psychologists tell us, for example, that a woman who turns up her palms is attracted to the man with whom she is speaking. (Don't you wish you'd known that in high school?) Prospective customers often signal their interest in doing business with us, so do some research to identify common clues. Choose a representative sample from among your best customers—perhaps 10, perhaps 100—and think back to when they were prospects. (You may need to talk to the salesperson who handled the individual accounts, or perhaps to the customers.) How did each one display interest? What were the earliest clues? How many times did you (or your rep) meet with him or her before closing a deal? What objections were raised, and how did you overcome them? What finally won over the customer? Write down as much information as you can remember. Your objective is to identify patterns of success that you can duplicate.

Outline your best way to find customers

Understanding how prospects behave lets you refine your firm's process for qualifying them. From the first time you target prospects, what steps do you take to close them? When do you use direct mail, advertising, telemarketing, and face-to-face selling? Is there a best way for your business to do this, or is it a random act? Match your tactics to the signals you get from prospects and identify the three most likely sequences that result in closing business. Are there predictable points where you and/or your prospects realize you aren't a good fit? Pin these scenarios down and think of ways to qualify prospects earlier in the process. Time is valuable for both of you.

Acquisition Sales Funnel

Suspects
Prospects
Qualified Prospects
Developed
Closed

Customize the categories for your funnel

Next, customize your funnel by organizing your findings. Define the markers your company will use to distinguish between each funnel stage. For example, you realize that a lot of your prospects are buying widgets from China, paying cheap prices but waiting weeks for shipments to arrive. A prospect who admits that the delay is hurting her business becomes a qualified prospect because she has expressed a pain that your business may (or may not) be able to resolve.

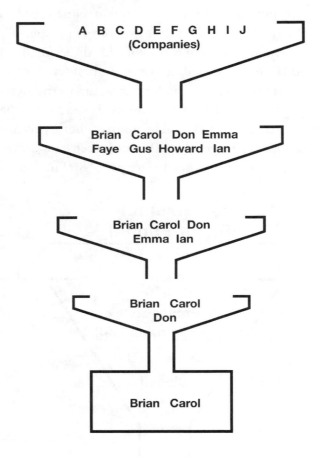

Add your own indicators to sharpen the definition of each of these funnel stages:

- A *suspect* is any company in your entire target market.
- A *prospect* is an identifiable decision maker within a company in your target market.
- A *qualified prospect* is a decision maker whom you determine has the time, need, authority, and money for your product or service.

- A *developed prospect* is a decision maker with the time, need, authority, and money for your product or service to whom you send a proposal, quote, or sample.
- A *closed prospect* is a decision maker who has agreed to make a purchase and whose check has cleared the bank.

As the previous figure shows, this can be as simple as plotting in points on a map. Set clear definitions so that you know exactly when a suspect (company) becomes a prospect (individual), then a qualified prospect, and so on. In this example, of the 10 companies listed, only five remain as "qualified prospects" because individuals within these companies have been identified as having time, need, authority, and money. (The other five may have been determined to be unqualified, or may still be in process.) Our hypothetical sales manager gets three of these five individuals to review a proposal, after which she closes two customers.

Small scale, yes, but the model makes the benefits of the funnel system transparent. Any company not within the seller's target market is disqualified from receiving sales and marketing resources, a potentially huge cost savings. Second, whoever is managing this prospect list can see at a glance how far each prospect has moved through the process. Because each category is matched with a set of activities, a sales associate knows *exactly which tactics* to apply to each buyer, *exactly which questions* to ask, and *exactly which objections* are likely to surface at a given point in time.

The more you work with the sales funnels, the more knowledge of customer behavior and expectations you will accrete. Try out different tactics to see which succeed cost-effectively. For example, if your staff makes costly personal visits to each prospect in your region, would a series of phone calls earn you just as many qualified prospects for a far lower cost?

☑ **Self-check: What is enough?**

Ebbs and flows in sales figures are to some extent inevitable, but you can protect yourself by keeping your acquisition funnel filled. Stay up to date about how many prospects you need at each stage and how much you can spend to move them through the funnel. The following formula will help you determine how many prospects you need at each stage:

1. Determine your average sale from a first-time buyer. For simplicity's sake, let's say it's $1,000.
2. Divide this number into your new customer sales goal to see how many first-time buyers you must land. If your goal is $10,000, then you must close 10 new buyers.
3. Move up the funnel to decide how many prospects you need at each step. If you typically close one buyer for each five qualified prospects, then you need at least 50 qualified prospects. Similarly, if you need to contact 50 suspects to identify one qualified prospect, don't plan on sleeping late until you identify 2,500 suspects or more.

Now that you know how many names you need at each funnel stage in order to meet your sales goal, it's time to figure out how much you can spend on them without breaking your bank. Complete these steps to figure out what your prospects are worth to you.

1. Divide the number of prospects it takes to close a sale into the value of the sale. If the average sale of a first-time buyer is $1,000, and if you must qualify five prospects to land one buyer, then each prospect generates $200 in revenue. Let's say it costs you about $100 to create those five prospects. Each prospect thus costs you $20.
2. Subtract the cost of a prospect—in this case, $20—from the revenue of a prospect; this gives you the *real value*. In our example, if you spend more than $180 trying to close each qualified prospect, you may hit your sales goal but flatten your margins.

Prospects with great potential for becoming long-term customers may be worth extra wooing and extra expenses, but this should be the exception. Figuring out the real value of a qualified prospect—or of a suspect, or of a prospect or developed prospect—gives you a benchmark of what to invest and what to expect in return. With financial guidelines in place, choose your tactics. Pick your sales, marketing, and customer service activities for each step of the funnel. Evaluate your activities, tools, and programs based on how cost effectively they deliver the numbers you need. Above all, focus on what matters—finding customers—rather than on tactics.

Retention
Sales Funnel

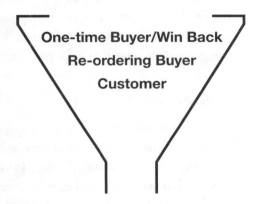

One-time Buyer/Win Back
Re-ordering Buyer
Customer

Marriage: The customer retention sales funnel

A nationally recognized lawn care corporation decided to break the backs of its Mom and Pop competitors by going after new business aggressively. By under-pricing smaller companies by as much as 50 percent, they doubled their local market share in just a few years.

Move over, local landscapers? Not quite. Although the corporation eliminated some competitors by "buying" their new customers, in terms of renewals, the corporation didn't do well. They weren't prepared to service—and weren't all that interested in servicing—the slew of new customers, who were used to the high quality service from local landscapers. The corporation invested way past the break-even point to win new business they couldn't keep. This reminds me of someone who marries his or her "first spouse" to see how things work out. It's legal, but it kind of misses the point of what marriage is all about.

The first product or service a new customer buys from your company is similar to this trial marriage; they want to see how things work out. There are plenty of fish in the sea, and new customers will start trawling unless you give them a reason to stay. Compared to prospecting, the customer retention phase typically costs you less money but more patience, personal attention, and routine care. Instant gratification—the *zing!* of signing a new buyer—is fleeting, so invest in your customers long-term by consistently setting, agreeing on, and meeting shared expectations.

Prospecting involves the thrill of the hunt, but customer retention is more like farming. You till the ground, work the soil, plant the seeds, trim the weeds, and eventually reap the harvest that will sustain you throughout a long, cold winter. Though less exciting, this stage promises deeper rewards.

Look for patterns of behavior

If you qualified your buyers well during the prospecting stage, their expectations should be in line with your firm's ability to deliver products and services. Beyond meeting these expectations, what do you do to nurture these new customers? Research your past successes at turning buyers into loyal customers. How did they gain confidence, recognize value, and build a continuing relationship with your business? Are there certain add-on services, for example, that you can offer at a predictable milestone, such as their second re-order? Look for patterns of what went right, and think about why.

Outline your best way of keeping customers

What is the first thing you do after you land a new buyer? Do you follow up? Do you have a predictable system for doing so? When do you use customer service, sales, telemarketing, and the Internet to foster relationships? Look at what is working and what you can improve, and write down the three most likely sequences of steps for developing buyers into loyal customers.

Customize the categories for your retention funnel

Organize your findings by describing the funnel terms based on common indicators for your company. Here are the stages of the retention funnel:

- A *one-time buyer* has chosen a low-risk way to "try out" your company, perhaps by selecting a single product or service.
- A *win-back buyer* has a previous, probably negative, experience with your company.
- A *reordering buyer* has made a passive decision to work with you again, but he or she is not yet loyal to your firm.
- A *customer* is married to your business.

Determine how much is enough

The self-check you did for the customer acquisition funnel can be applied to the retention funnel so you can figure out how many you need and how much you can spend at each stage. Let's update it in terms of keeping customers.

- Determine your average sale from a stable customer ($1,000).
- Divide this number into your sales goal from retained customers ($10,000) to get the number of stable customers you must land (10).
- Move up the funnel and decide how many buyers you must attract at each step.
- Now divide the number of one-time buyers it takes to create a stable customer into the value of a stable customer. For example, if your average sale from a stable customer is worth $4,000 and you need four first-time buyers to create a stable customer, then a first-time buyer generates $1,000 of revenue. This is your benchmark for knowing how much to invest in developing a buyer into a customer.

With a grasp of the numbers, you can pick the most effective sales, marketing, and customer service activities for each step of the retention funnel. Track which ones deliver the numbers you need at the price you want to invest, and make adjustments when necessary.

Let it ride

The secret to keeping customers can be summed up in the word "consistency." People want to feel secure, and they don't want to have to think too hard about things that can be made routine. This is a great opportunity for us as owners to make it safer and easier for our customers to stay.

When I was a product manager at the Bank of Boston, we had a group of customers who had collectively deposited over $50 million in non-interest bearing savings accounts. They neither complained nor moved their money. When I expressed my astonishment to our bank president, he said, "Inertia is our best friend. If there is ever a problem with these accounts, we will drop what we are doing to resolve it before the customers know it has happened." And he was right. Unless forced to pay attention, these customers were content to go on with their lives and enrich the bank at their own expense. Did we do wrong by those customers? Not in their minds. The moral of the story is this: a stable customer has certain expectations that have been set and must be met. If you disturb their ability to do business in the most passive way, you risk losing their business. Because reordering customers offer the most profit to your firm, why ever would you try?

Raising Children: The customer development sales funnel

Marriage counselors claim that the most successful unions occur between two people with similar backgrounds but divergent interests. This attests to the importance of shared goals and ways of thinking as well as to the spark created by seeking out new experiences. As the needs of mates change over time, their similarities bind them, and their differences keep things interesting.

In business, your goal with loyal customers should be to build a deep, mutually beneficial bond, like the one that grows between long-married partners, particularly those who have children. If "new experiences" are important to keeping a marriage happy, kids certainly qualify! Even strong relationships go through periods of adjustment when a baby comes along, and everything is complicated. The initial roles of husband and wife are overwhelmed, and a new, deeper relationship begins taking shape.

You want to develop a deep connection with your customers but without the dirty diapers, right? I call this process of customer development "growing champions" because these are the true advocates of your firm. As you pass through various stages of your business life, these are partners who help when necessary and accept help when offered. Your relationships with your champions are simultaneously selfish and selfless: selfish because this marriage benefits both of you, but selfless because you would risk a lot, and give a lot, to keep the partnership going. Doesn't this sound similar to parenting? The pride you take in your daughter's nose is pure narcissism (it looks exactly like yours) but for how many other people would you sacrifice your life? The love we feel for our children, similar to the love we express for our parents, is the purest form of love most of us will ever know.

Birol's bit: Trust trumps trepidation

Financial service providers recognize business owners for the potential cash cows we are. Life insurance, SEP-IRAs, tax preparation—added to the basic menu of such lucrative specials as general accounting, payroll management, investment advising, buy-sell and key man agreements, and tax avoidance products—and who wouldn't love us? But what would it take for a service provider to convince you to put all your financial eggs in one basket? Faith in his or her abilities, right? Plus a rock-solid belief in his or her integrity.

Let's begin with a single purchase, perhaps LTD insurance. The advisor seems nice, and when you open an IRA several weeks later, you listen to her stock picks. When her fund of choice rockets up 10 percent, you arrange to buy some shares. By the time she asks for a meeting to explain her comprehensive financial management package, you've almost doubled your investment.

How likely are you to sign up with this provider? Hey, she has compiled a track record and gained your trust. You are on your way to becoming an advocate for her firm. After all, if you have a crackerjack accountant—or hair stylist, dentist, virtual assistant, or babysitter—you probably sing their praises all around town.

Deep, long-term customer relationships are interdependent and mutually beneficial. Though your investment will probably be higher than the retention stage, growing champions is cheaper than prospecting because you focus on a few, quality individuals. In the retention stage, you must make it easier for customers to stay than to go, but in the development stage, you must make the idea of their leaving *unthinkable*.

Look for patterns of behavior

How do your better customers adapt your products and services to suit their needs? Do those customer relationships resemble partnerships or strategic alliances? Look for successful patterns you can duplicate.

Outline your process for growing champions

Identify the milestones that bring customers closer to your firm. At what point do you begin to involve them in new product development or customer councils? What led to this point? When do you first ask, and when do you receive, referrals and references? Plot out the three most likely sequences for growing champions.

Customize each funnel stage

What are the initial milestones that increase a buyer's dependency on your business? Common ones include a third purchase or the exchange of previously withheld information. Identify these milestones and create definitions for each of these terms:

- A *stable customer* is one who has passed the milestone(s) identified above.
- A *cross-sold* or *up-sold* customer buys multiple products or services and agrees to participate in customer councils, strategic alliances, or the testing of new products.
- A *champion/advocate* is a customer who gladly gives you references and provides you with ongoing referrals. Champions confer exponential value on your firm.

Development
Sales Funnel

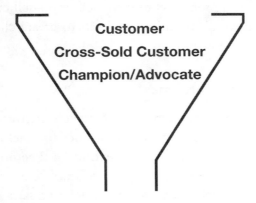

Customer

Cross-Sold Customer

Champion/Advocate

Determine how much is enough

Using the same formula as for the acquisition and retention funnels, figure out how many champions you need and what you can spend to get them. Follow these steps:

- Divide your average sale from a customer into the total sales you expect from champions. This gives you the number of champions you must land.
- Determine how many customers you need at each step to meet this goal. If you qualify three cross-sold or up-sold customers for each champion, then plan to do so.
- Divide the number of customers it takes to create a champion into the revenue of a champion. Thus, if you need five customers to create a champion who generates $50,000 of revenue, each customer represents $10,000 of potential revenue. If you must spend $5,000 to create a champion, you can spend up to $1,000 cultivating each customer.
- By subtracting the cost of developing five customers (here, $5,000) from the revenue of a champion ($50,000) you have the real value of a champion ($45,000).

Create champions effectively

With financial guidelines in place, pick your most effective sales, marketing, and customer service activities for each step of the funnel. For instance, consider using seminars to cross-sell or up-sell customers while emphasizing executive tours and referral kits to create champions. Keep your eye on costs and success rates.

One process, three outcomes

You probably noticed the repetition between the three sales funnels. Although the definitions and goals are distinct for each, the process is duplicable no matter whether you are finding, keeping, or growing customers. This simplicity is powerful. In contrast to a catchy marketing campaign, a pitch by a young ad agency, a weeklong sales retreat for your staff, or a super-efficient and super-expensive CRM suite, the funnels won't pretend to do your work for you. So, don't fool yourself. Plot out what you need to do to grow your business—then start doing it!

Trigger events

There is that moment in a new relationship when two people, formerly strangers, share an expectation of being together every Saturday night. The new toothbrush in the medicine cabinet; brunch with the parents; wandering together into a jewelry store and ending up in front of the diamond rings. Coincidence? No. It's a trigger event.

Trigger events signify relationship milestones. In terms of prospects and customers, we can locate common triggers in order to predict behavior and offer the customer what they need when they are ready. Common trigger events include:

- The third sale.
- The second problem (resolved to satisfaction).
- The fourth reorder.
- The third season.
- The second referral.

These vary by industry, so you may find a different pattern with your customers. Study your data and nail down typical buying patterns. Begin by defining which products or services:

- New buyers are likely to choose first.
- Encourage the most return purchases.
- Are one-time impulse buys.
- Are most popular with existing customers.

Look at how telephone companies mass-market long-distance deals to attract first-time buyers, and then lock them in to a long-term commitment with "Friends and Family" plans. Cool phone equipment, such as caller ID boxes or Mickey Mouse phones, are impulse buys that must be instantly profitable for the seller, but peddling personal 800 numbers, automated voice mail, and DSL (often packaged) to existing customers is like hitting the mother lode.

Final thoughts

The three sales funnels make up a natural system of checks and balances similar to the executive, legislative, and judicial branches of our government. For example, if your development funnel is full, your retention funnel is half-full, and your acquisition funnel is more than half-empty, you know it's time to focus on prospecting!

Every business experiences bottlenecks. Some companies struggle to generate qualified prospects, others can't close them, and still others can't keep or grow the customers they have. By laying out all the information in the three funnels, you can spot problems on paper before they develop in real life. Use these tools to align activities, reconcile costs, and assure that the cost, number, velocity, and flow of prospects at each stage of your sales cycle is predictable and sufficient, in both *quality* and *quantity*, for your sales forecast and business needs.

As anyone who watched the *Sopranos,* the *Apprentice,* or *Dynasty* knows, business is all about relationships. Thinking about the end result of dating, marriage, and parenting as a metaphor for finding, keeping, and growing customers can put your efforts into context. All three are critical, for a business that enjoys stable, rapid, profitable growth is one that has mastered these three divergent phases that occur congruently. From the thrill of landing new clients, to the security of strong relationships, to the fulfillment of interdependence, your philosophy of growth should be consistent. Tactics, programs, and results will come and go, but the goals of finding, keeping, and growing customers provide the foundation for everything we do.

☑   Self-check: Give me a CRM

Business is all about relationships, which is why Customer Relationship Management software is so appealing. CRM packages (now called suites) can integrate the functions, activities, tactics, and programs that comprise a company's sales, marketing, and customer service departments. They let you bond on autopilot—sort of like hiring a personal assistant to buy gifts for your spouse—and therein lies the problem. Despite all the hype about CRM, business owners must proceed with caution. CRM solutions are only as good as the manual systems they automate, and some are more advanced than small and middle-market companies need. CRM suites are *not* marketing solutions, nor are they the ultimate answer to sales growth.

CRM suites are great for managing customer databases built with your sales funnels. Just don't commit before your company is ready. Here are some tips for deciding when it's time to use a CRM:

- You have developed and implemented a process for how your business finds, keeps, and grows its customers.
- Your system works manually, but your business is outgrowing it.
- Your existing customer data is useful and up to date and ready to be transferred to the CRM.
- Your staff agrees on what it needs from a CRM suite, not what would be really cool to play around with.
- You have built your plan before talking to a technology vendor or consultant. This will help you avoid buying more CRM than your business requires.
- You have defined a clear Return On Investment (ROI) for the project and have planned on spending three dollars in training and implementation for every dollar in hardware and software.

Chapter 4

To Market, to Market: Tending your systems for fulfillment and delivery

The world loves underdogs and rebels who talk big and then come through. There are plenty of role models out there, but my favorites are two guys who started out in the 1960s, one a college drop-out and the other just plain trouble. But when Mick Jagger and Keith Richards joined their musical, promotional, and business talents, the small ultimate business survival story was born.

The Rolling Stones have staged so many comebacks and delivered on so many wild prognostications that they have been featured on the cover of *Fortune* magazine and Sir Mick has been knighted by the Queen of England. Why bring up the Stones when we are talking small business? Because they built a concert, musical, and merchandizing empire that probably dwarfs the royalties they earn for writing and playing music.

Generally acknowledged as the world's greatest rock and roll band, the Rolling Stones—on the fast track to becoming septuagenarians—are going on tour again. They certainly haven't gathered much moss!

Delivering Best and Highest Use

One of the great challenges for any business is to keep rocking and rolling past the stage of youthful vigor into middle age and beyond. You have honed your Best and Highest Use and you know how to find, keep, and grow more customers. Although periodic renewals of passion and reassessments of processes are critical, you have moved into a new stage of the game in which delivering on what your company sells is your primary challenge.

Owners from a sales background need to realize that at some point they must stop "faking it until they start making it." For others, especially owners from the engineering or development side, the test is to make sure the company is delivering not at the top of its capabilities but at the top level of what its customers will pay for. In either case, the business owner must learn to get the goods to market in a way that keeps the company profitable, healthy, and growing. Nowhere does this have more impact than in the areas of fulfillment and production.

What could your business achieve by leveraging its Best and Highest Use in every imaginable way to deliver on its customers' desire for its products and services? This is art and science, the marriage of the purely creative with the eminently practical (and profitable). It is also one of the toughest transitions any entrepreneur must make. But really, it's pretty simple. You must focus on three fundamentals:

- The customer expectations that you and your customers agree on.
- The impact (real value) of your service on your customers' business results on you and your business.
- Your firm's true cost and opportunity cost of meeting expectations and delivering real value to your customers.

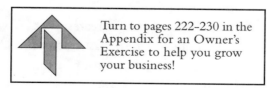

Turn to pages 222–230 in the Appendix for an Owner's Exercise to help you grow your business!

The key in integrating these somewhat conflicting measures is to create a staircase of delivery and fulfillment by offering different levels of product-service combinations to meet different customer needs, and requiring customers to pay for whichever level they choose.

Setting and meeting customer expectations

In the business world, communication problems are the primary cause of break-ups. Of companies that fail, customer relationships that end, and employees who are fired, the majority are caused by the failure to set and then meet expectations with the other party. Perhaps the most common error we owners make is to sell shovels when customers really want holes. This is a classic example of product versus benefits, where the communications lines between the customer and the business can become confused. We get wrapped up in all that we can do, what we can provide, and how we can excel, and forget to find out whether any of it is what the customer really wants. Customers are pragmatic. If you understand their pain and resolve it, or see their opportunity and help them take it, and they will keep coming back.

Tiers of service

One of the best ways to communicate and agree upon expectations and performance measurement is to make your contract transparent. You can do this by creating tiers—basically "packages" or bundles of products and services—to provide various levels of value at specific price points. Customers who value cost savings over convenience have the option of choosing a basic package at a low price; your firm keeps the sale but is free of any obligation to provide heroic service or repairs *because the customer chose not to pay for them.*

These basic or trial packages are good ways to get prospects to test your firm. You can gradually work them up to higher tiers as their dependence on your firm increases. Thus, the tiers act as a guide for moving customers through the retention and development sales funnels, creating champions and augmenting profits. (This can be extremely effective if you tie your sales staff's compensation to the packages they sell.)

One of the best examples of tiered pricing is Continental Airline's One Pass Program, with its Silver, Gold, and Platinum designations targeted toward returning customers, specifically business travelers. Hey, the only people who don't hate flying are those who hardly ever do it. With One Pass, Continental has found a way to resolve customer pain and create its own opportunity by offering desirable upgrades to frequent travelers—for a price.

For example, by offering mileage bonuses to customers who buy tickets online, Continental bypasses the cost of travel agents. Customer loyalty is fostered through the Elite Program, which grants low-cost rewards such as priority seating, priority baggage handling, and airport security access to frequent flyers. By making Elite passengers compete for upgrades (first class, aisle seat, emergency row), the airline has enhanced the value of its premium offerings, creating a hierarchy of benefits for its most loyal, highest-paying customers. And at a time when the travel industry as a whole is slumping, Continental supplements its revenue through selling airline club memberships, airport limousine services, and even air alternatives such as train travel, all fueled by the dangling carrot of more airline points and perks. What a wonderful way to modify customer behavior in ways that improve the company's ability to operate efficiently and profitably.

Delivering value

Setting and meeting customer expectations goes a long way toward providing value for your customers. When you understand their pain and opportunity, you will discover new and better ways to serve them and increase their loyalty to your firm, and save your company the cost of delivering extras that customers don't value.

This is a matter of quality versus quantity, or, to put it another way, of giving a loved one the gift he or she wants rather than the one you feel like giving. The U.S. economy, particularly the manufacturing sector, has responded to recent challenges with cries for better customer service and quality control, with the result, ironically, that more businesses are disconnected from their customers than ever before. How can this be? Too many companies have slipped into the trap of giving customers what *they* think customers should want. It doesn't do much good to write a mission statement about "exceeding customer expectations" if you don't know what those expectations are! Remember that a customer won't buy your shovel if he or she is not interested in the ultimate benefit of having a shovel: a hole.

Key catalyst: Delivery

To succeed long-term, your business must run like a well-oiled machine, providing more of your output to more customers as profitably as possible. Whether you manufacture and deliver products, distribute wholesale or retail products made by other companies, or provide personal or professional services, the delivery process that has served you well so far is probably outdated.

Businesses at the $5 million to $20 million level need cash, and it is always preferable to have customers fund your growth than to seek investors. Think of the difference in motives. Customers want your company to succeed because they benefit from the value it provides, while investors simply want to profit by flipping your company to other investors.

Delivery and fulfillment represent the key catalyst at this level because they directly impact customer happiness, which translates into sales, which fuel future growth, which allows you to deliver increased value to customers, continuing the cycle at ever higher levels.

Scaling up your Best and Highest Use is key to providing more of your output to more customers in ways they will pay for. Here are four steps to get you started:

1. Understand your company's BHU and deliver it as effectively as possible.
2. Determine how you will change the distribution of more of your products and services to serve increasing numbers of new buyers.

3. Restructure or develop new mechanisms for increasing your delivery.
4. Develop a system to scale up or replicate your new delivery.

Step 1: Enhancing BHU

Make the most of what you have without dramatically increasing your overhead or fixed costs by squeezing every last drop from your BHU. First, determine what your customers are *truly* paying you for. What is their expected outcome? What benefits are they looking for? Next, understand your current capacity and production costs as much as possible, while using your existing system. This will differ depending on your type of business. These are the four types of business. Decide which one describes your company best, and then apply the skills to enhance your BHU.

- *Personal or professional services.* Focus on the results your services create. Focus on coverage your services provide or assurance that your product or service can offer, and sell a greater capacity at a lower cost.
- *Distributing or wholesaling.* Provide your vendor with coverage, reports, and commitments for volume. Expand your coverage by drop-shipping more products.
- *Manufacturing.* Focus on quality, timeliness, and support. Run three shifts and outsource lower value-added services rather than building more space or adding more workers.
- *Retailing.* Provide value-added services to your customers and product suggestions and sales information to your vendors. Increase your hours, sell more online, and have your vendors deliver more items before you add costly inventory.

Step 2: Adjust distribution for greater volume

Determine how you will change the distribution of more of your products and services to serve increasing numbers of new buyers. It's important to understand the three drivers of scaling up: size, time, and location. Size is the impact of producing, coordinating, and sequencing more products and services, and time involves both the additional elapsed time it takes to produce, apply, and deliver larger orders to greater numbers of customers as well as the increased frequency of doing so.

Finally, location represents the challenge of selling, delivering, and servicing in multiple or larger locations. As you produce more, how will you get it to customers? You might change your reach from local to regional, for example, or your delivery from in-house to outsourced.

A third option is to adjust the format by delivering in different quantities or packaging products and services more efficiently. Again, the specifics depend on the type of business you run. Here are a few examples of the things you can do to enhance your BHU for great volume:

- *For personal or professional services:* How will you supervise and house the extra people you need? What do they need in order to work effectively and efficiently at their jobs? As you expand your distribution, consider the impact of distance and consistency. For example, if you provide out of town services, sell them in daylong increments or via phone or teleconference sessions.

- *For distributing or wholesaling products:* Focus on order size, delivery standards, and where and how you receive, transfer, and deliver your goods. Consider the impact that outsourcing, expectations, and human relations have on your business.

- *For manufacturing:* Identify the direct and indirect costs of adding capacity. Your overhead costs and efficiencies are likely to behave in unknown ways, particularly when you increase SKUs (stock keeping units) as well as volume. As your marketing department demands additional colors, sizes, quantities, and versions of your product, pay attention to your gross margins. Your profit margins must more than make up for the increased costs and probable losses in economies of scale.

- *For retailing:* Focus on your customers. Remember that your "open to buy" and "beat yesterday" systems move directly with what you are selling, and yesterday's profits must cover tomorrow's inventory. Your approach to depth, breadth, and width of products carried, as well as staffing, will critically impact your costs, performance, and efficiencies.

Step 3: Restructure the system to work for you

You need to develop new mechanism: for increasing your delivery. Begin by identifying the critical inputs in your business. Do you have the time, knowledge, raw materials, money, and people in the right places, quantities, and configuration?

- *For personal or professional services*: Maintain quality of output and assurance measured in the eyes of the consumer.
- *For distributing or wholesaling*: Maintain consistency of delivery times, customer services, and information processing. Customers require consistency in billing, invoicing, ordering, and the identification and resolution of problems.
- *For manufacturing*: Focus on implementing lean manufacturing, theory of constraints, and critical standards such as Six Sigma.
- *For retailing*: Increase stockturns (avoiding stockouts) and assure your premium items are available from both primary and backup vendors.

Step 4: Develop a system to scale up delivery

In working to this point, you will gain a better understanding of the resource needs, procedures, and limits of your new increased system. Here are the appropriate actions to take for each type of business:

- *For personal or professional services*: Recruit, manage, and develop the right people. Give them tools and procedures to maintain standards and customer satisfaction. Recognize when your methods of control are stretched and create new ones flexible enough to work at higher levels of personal productivity.
- *For distributing or wholesaling*: Create a system that knows how much of a given product will need to be available. What will it cost you? How will you respond to exceptions, mistakes, and other unexpected events?
- *For manufacturing*: Focus on maintaining consistency in quality, delivery, and costs regardless of how volume, versions, and inventory levels are increased. As variability is introduced into your shop floor, margins must continue to grow at least as much to make up for the economies of scale you will certainly lose.

- *For retailing:* Keep a consistent stock of core items, those things that 80 percent of your customers want. As you add more goods, use the traditional tools of "beat yesterday" and your "open-to-buy" systems to ensure that you have the money to spend on replenishing your stock. Also, make sure that your systems have the ability to manage your stock turns, and that your Human Resources policies encourage the customer-focused staff you need.

As you grow, keep your eye on your new, expanding limits, and don't overstep them. Most importantly, stick to your core objectives, whether you are serving one customer, or one million.

Covering your costs

In developing your delivery system, you can choose one of three basic options as your model. In an *on-demand* system, the customer can have anything and everything anytime and anywhere. The customer is buying your commitment to providing products and services as she requires them, so customers with deep pockets typically appreciate this level of service. Your firm can benefit from the steady income stream, but you must be careful not to over-commit your resources at any given time. This method can be too pricey and/or too comprehensive for some customers, depending on their level of need.

In contrast, a *pay-as-you-go* system is more like grocery shopping; as the customer wanders down each aisle, he or she picks and chooses products and services according to the demand and timetable. While you need to set your price high enough to cover your costs, because the customer's behavior isn't entirely predictable, your business may have trouble achieving a steady income stream.

The third option is a blend of on-demand and pay-as-you-go. The customer makes enough commitment to you to enable you to deliver most profitably, yet he is not locked into a specific volume or payment schedule. This model satisfies a customer's need for flexibility and control while keeping your profits healthy. Whichever method you choose—and many companies offer versions of each—keep the focus on *maximizing your sales and profits* along with your customer's perception of value. This is the only way you can truly work to enhance your BHU and maximize your profits without risk.

Pricing and control

One of the most important and elusive aspects of fulfillment and delivery involves pricing. Certain products and services are inelastic in terms of price, meaning that fluctuations have little to no effect on consumer behavior. If what you sell is inelastic, slashing prices will cut your profits without changing customer behavior.

On the other hand, some products are highly elastic. Today's newspaper contains an advertisement by a travel company offering a week's stay at an all-inclusive resort in Cabo San Lucas (including airfare) for $799 per person. Suddenly, you're thinking about a vacation!

How do you know when a price is right? Let's say that you meet a prospect for lunch in an attempt to close a deal. When you finally come to the point of stating your price, one of three things happens:

- Your prospect immediately says no, stands, and walks away.
- Your prospect immediately says yes, shakes your hand, and treats you, the waiter, and everyone at the surrounding tables to champagne.
- Your prospect contemplates the offer. The long silence feels like an ocean in your head until you hear that magical word: Yes!

In two of the three situations, you closed the deal, but only in the third have you done it right. If the prospect rejects the offer out of hand, he believes the price is too high, which means that you have failed to sell the benefits of what your company provides. If the prospect takes the offer immediately, you have given away too much value for too low a price. You know you've got it right when your prospect accepts your offer only after some deliberation. In this case, he knows the value he is losing if he says no.

Birol's bit: Cruising along

The cruise business is a great example of aligning customer expectations, economic reality, and the cost of delivering unforgettable experiences to unrealistic consumers. As an officer on a Holland America ship put it to me, "The less people pay, the more they demand." How does a high-cost, high-capacity business deliver profitably when customers expect too much? Holland America has achieved a 70 percent returning passenger rate by:

- Creating multiple levels of passenger rooms and personal service with a goal of breaking even on the cruise tickets while profiting from onboard services, products, and add-ons such as alcohol, trips, photographs, and gambling.
- Creating a preferred vendor program whereby island stores pay the company to send customers their way.
- Providing an unlimited amount of a relatively low-cost resource: food. The more people eat, the more they need to drink, and Holland America profits nicely from the sale of alcohol.

Of course, these activities would mean little if the company failed to deliver what customers want from a cruise—a culture of romance, experience, and freedom. Similar to most large organizations, Holland America must be careful not to stray too far from its Best and Highest Use of providing an extraordinary cruise ship experience.

Delivery for dummies

There is one sure way to know whether your delivery system is working. Do customers agree to act as references for your firm? Do they willingly provide you with referrals? If so, you are delivering value and providing good customer service. Assuming your margins are also healthy, you're in business!

While this definition may seem trite, it creates an important financial connection. Take your total investment in customer service and divide it by the value of incremental referrals, references, and sales traceable to that investment. This will give you a ballpark cost and value.

References and referrals are the proof that you are giving customers what they want. Anything else is just lip service. If you are creating this level of customer loyalty without having to put people in strangleholds, your delivery system is on the right track. Don't try to "exceed expectations." Instead, be consistent in what you currently deliver and grow your customers' expectations to a higher level when it will benefit both of your firms.

Delivering on your Best and Highest Use means co-opting your customer's expectations, behavior, and payment references so that they work for your firm. Keep control of the purse strings while giving customers the perception of control and flexibility in getting what they want, when they want it. And sell each buyer to the highest tier that meets his or her definitions of value and acceptable price.

☑ Self-check: Send in the clowns

If you often feel as if you are running a three-ring circus, you aren't far off. Any business, whether it's a service, manufacturing, retail, or distribution firm, must distill all day-to-day efforts into three areas—selling, delivering, and developing—and keep all three spinning at the same time. Even if you accomplish two and neglect only one, you are letting down the audience at that end of the tent, and your business will suffer. For example:

- *Sell and deliver*? Your firm will continue living hand–to–mouth until you develop your brand.
- *Sell and develop*? You will build a reputation for flashy marketing and empty promises, as the poor value of your products and services drive customers away.
- *Deliver and develop*? Your existing customers better really, really like you because you won't be bringing in new business.

Of the three activities, *selling* has the potential for the greatest short–term impact. Selling starts and keeps your company rolling, so you need to focus on the concepts of pain and opportunity. For example:

- ☐ Do you know what customer pain your company helps resolve?
- ☐ Do you know what opportunity you help customers gain?
- ☐ Do you know how to tell and sell the difference?

As an owner, you are also sales associate number one for your firm, whether you are in the trenches signing deals or building a stellar reputation and imparting wisdom, your sales efforts are effective when you propose to three of every 10 prospects you meet and close one of the three.

While you are selling, you also must deliver what you like making in a way that meets your customers' expectations. For example:

- ☐ Do you know at least 10 different ways your firm's BHU meets your clients' needs?
- ☐ Do you know at least 10 different questions to ask about how to meet their needs?
- ☐ Do you know at least three reasons why customers keep ordering from you?
- ☐ Do you know at least three reasons why some customers don't keep ordering from you?

Determine your Best and Highest Use and assure it continues to meet your client's needs. As your perception of your customers' pain and opportunity and your firm's ability to resolve them grows, your target market will narrow, making it easier to keep all three rings in motion. By focusing on selling, delivering, and developing your company at the same time, you will be focusing on the right company goals. Selling solves your short-term revenue needs, delivering ensures that you exchange value for money, and development means you continually build and fortify your growing brand. If you do any two and neglect the third, your business will suffer.

Chapter 5

Keep On Keepin' On:
Repetition and consistency
for stable growth

In the Rock and Roll Hall of Fame, one of my favorite exhibits is called *One Hit Wonders*. Full of artists and songs such as the Starland Vocal Band's "Afternoon Delight" and The Archie's "Sugar Sugar," it is a veritable *Who's Who* of what could have been. So goes business. Many small companies and their owners shine brightly for awhile, earning the label of shooting star, but sputter out and never fulfill their early promise. Typically this happens because the owners can't (or don't want to) capture and cement their successful practices.

Then there are the businesses and owners who break our professional hearts, whose reprehensible behavior torpedoes years of investment and customer loyalty. In the face of dirty dealing, fallen idols, and self-destructive greed, big business has accounted for some major scandals, and employees, retirees, shareholders, and taxpayers have paid the price. Meanwhile, most of us long for—and often operate in—a different kind of business world, one built on relationships of mutual trust and mutual benefits between companies and their stakeholders.

The bigger your company, the more likely you are to be tarred with the brush of suspicion created by the recent scandals. The deep pockets of large companies can often substitute for trust and honest deal-making, but few entrepreneurs or smaller companies can survive without establishing and honoring relationships. This is a great untold story of American business. While multi-nationals have unlimited resources and political influence, business owners have the great advantage of building strong connections through personal attention and consistency. Huge companies must resort to buying loyalty, but small businesses can earn it one client at a time.

In previous chapters we talked a lot about customers: understanding their needs, targeting those who need us, delivering our Best and Highest Use to resolve their pain or to create opportunity for them. Now we turn to the fifth and final catalyst of seven-figure growth: repetition and consistency. They are the ultimate consequences of using your passion, BHU, and sales, marketing, and delivery methods to achieve your goal of stable and profitable growth. What do I mean by repetition and consistency? Driven by your passion and guided by your BHU, you develop effective systems for finding, keeping, and growing customers. Profitable growth is simply a matter of doing all the right things over and over again.

Each success will boost your sense of confidence, competence, and conviction while enhancing your firm's reputation. Unlike the large company that spends its way into the hearts and minds of customers, you have an opportunity to *walk your own talk*. Customers, employees, and vendors will see you keeping promises and making progress in a consistent manner. This is where trust and relationships are cemented.

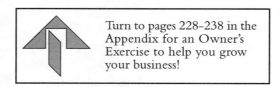

Turn to pages 228–238 in the Appendix for an Owner's Exercise to help you grow your business!

Consistency builds your brand

Similar to big companies, good small businesses develop a presence in their marketplace. When this is done really well, a company of any size can create an identity that surpasses what they were originally selling. Remember when Martha Stewart was known for her recipes and crafts? Now she is a lifestyle, an icon of women in business, and, after her latest trials, a survivor. Small and mid-sized firms can achieve brands as effective as Martha's in their own corner of the market.

Your brand is your commitment to customers, employees, and suppliers, and of course, your banker. Nothing is more important than delivering on your promises. The good news is that this doesn't cost you anything! Even on a tight budget, you can brand your company in a few simple ways:

- Build your offer, your marketing, and your brand around your company's BHU and leverage it through value-added products and services.
- Outsource or delegate everything not related to your BHU.
- Tell your story well in order to market yourself and your company on a personal level.
- Communicate your message through all affordable means, including electronic resources, ink on paper, at live gatherings, and through any other venues you can find.

Birol's bit: Bucks versus basics

With millions of dollars to buy celebrity spokespeople and air time for Michael, Serena, Venus, and Tiger, the Nike Corporation has managed one of the great sleights of hand in modern marketing. The truth behind the ubiquitous swoosh? It's a *checkmark*, people!

If you aren't already striving to provide excellent and consistent delivery, an expensive marketing campaign won't save you. Even Nike couldn't stay profitable if they routinely stiffed their vendors or retailers, or sold their customers inferior shoes.

By establishing a recognizable brand, you will lower your costs of finding customers in terms of money, time, and energy; avoid closing customers who sap your profits; and create a referral network to do your prospecting for you. I once stayed in an upscale hotel that promoted its restaurant and bar by taping a note underneath the toilet seat in each guest room: "Look under your potty to get a free toddy." Guess what? I went down for my toddy and ended up eating most of my meals there for the next few days. So, I ask you, how far is too far? Keep looking for opportunities!

Owning your market

Subtle sponsorship has gone the way of Three Rivers Stadium and Candlestick Park. From golf tournaments to customer awards to publicity-getting reports on products, services, or industry trends, there are as many ways to get noticed as there are people willing to sell advertising space on their foreheads. For example, watch any televised sporting event and take note of how many companies generously provide you with a score rundown, a slow-motion replay, or a half-time "million dollar shot" that an Average Joe misses by a mile. Sometimes this works, but sometimes it doesn't.

Plastering a company's name all around town (or all over the airwaves) builds recognition, but to own a piece of your industry, you must offer a sample of your BHU. Many companies partially sponsor trade shows in ways that highlight their expertise. For example, at a regional electronics fair, a health maintenance organization might host informational sessions on preventive medicine and safety in the workplace. Your efforts don't need to be elaborate. Publish a monthly e-newsletter that emphasizes information over promotion, or write guest columns for a local newspaper. Put together a seminar for prospects and customers on a topic that melds your expertise with their needs.

Client case study: FlorLine Midwest

As any parent knows, a 20-year old boy isn't necessarily as mature as he sounds. Hidden inside that 6-foot tall, 220 pound body is the chaotic mind of a frat boy. Similarly, years of experience and growing sales don't guarantee that a business is "all grown up." Founder Chris Reynolds and his partner (and brother) Shane readily admit that after 20 years of building FlorLine Midwest, their internal processes were more like an awkward teenager than a titan of industry.

FlorLine, based in Massillon, Ohio, is a contractor of high-performance flooring and wall systems that accounts for more than 30-million square feet of flooring throughout the eastern United States. The company's roster of past and current clients boasts such corporate giants as Coca-Cola, Nabisco, Honda, Pfizer, and Nissan, and by its twentieth year in business, FlorLine was serving companies in 30 states, mostly in the manufacturing, biomedical, and food and beverage industries. Chris and Shane never had trouble finding customers and making sales, but by 2003 their gross margins were in decline. "We had grown fast but not smart, and we didn't really have the systems in place to allow us to grow properly," Shane acknowledged, adding, "We didn't have much of a system at all."

When Shane and I met during a national sales meeting hosted by the Garland Floor Company, a FlorLine supplier and client of Birol Growth Consulting, we discussed some ideas for focusing his company, which was already doing well, with growth up about 30 percent over the year before. FlorLine was an example of a good company that was hitting a glass ceiling because it didn't have the systems in place for sustained, rapid growth. "The tendency for a lot of people is to wait until times get bad before they turn to a consultant," Shane said, "but we wanted to position ourselves to take better advantage of our opportunities. Even when you're succeeding, there's always room to grow."

With that kind of commitment from a client, I knew this would be an enjoyable experience. Because the Reynolds brothers—like many owners— were experts in their industry but not in business development, they hired me to give the firm direction and brought in a new employee, Bill Moul, to manage their efforts. The four of us got to work on the sales funnels to identify suspects, prospects, and customers, and devise methods to improve profitability. We gave shape to the company's random way of finding customers by creating three categories of prospects:

- *Blind Bid*: Public bid opportunities decided solely on price, with no opportunity for the company to distinguish its Best and Highest Use. According to Shane, these were "high volume, less margins, and more headaches" accounts.
- *Lead Generated*: Referrals made by manufacturers, current customers, or reps who matched a prospect's needs to FlorLine's capabilities. Although profit margins were better, these accounts demanded a lot of attention and time.
- *Relationship Sales*: Any past or current customer of FlorLine represented a potential relationship sale. Profit margins were high because satisfied customers were often willing to pay premium prices for quality and service they could trust.

I assigned Bill and Shane the task of setting specific targets, based on annual percentage growth, for each category of customers with the overall objective being increased margins. After they set the final numbers—25 percent for Blind Bid; 25 percent for Lead Generated; and 50 percent for Customer Relationships—we defined sales tactics for each account type. To increase profitability, the company had to find a message that communicated what its relationship customers wanted—an efficient, reliable way to purchase quality floors and wall systems. The company's old tag line—"A leader in design and application of protective coating systems"— was plain-spoken to a fault, so the company redesigned all its literature, including letterheads, marketing materials, and the Website, to highlight its appeal to customers. The result? A new message that speaks directly to what customers want: *FlorLine Quality: Increasing Productivity and Reducing Risk for Over 20 Years.*

According to Shane Reynolds, FlorLine now has a "whole new way of selling" the business. "We've gained a deeper understanding of our own company, and for the first time, we understand what our best customers are really buying, and how to sell them what they want."

Consistency begins with BHU

Developing your company's long-term ability to perform at higher levels involves refining what you've already done, and the more consistent your efforts are, the more you will learn about your recipe for success. Understand what it takes to develop prospects and build the top half of your sales funnel: brand what you sell while continuing to distill and expand your and your company's BHU, narrow your target market, and pursue greater opportunities to resolve customer pain and seize opportunities to grow their business. In other words, do everything you are doing—just keep doing it better.

Reinvigorate your conviction

From my experiences in raising a disabled child who has random hospital stays and chronic medical challenges, I have learned to make hay while our sun is shining. My daughter, Margo, is a constant reminder of what strength and determination can accomplish, and she makes it impossible for my wife and me to get too wrapped up in things that aren't important. Put simply, she has brought a lot of pain into our lives—anyone who has seen his or her child lying in an intensive care unit will know what I mean—but the pain is far outweighed by joy.

Too often companies let their failures, legacies, or challenges overwhelm their totally justifiable sense of confidence and conviction; bad times are seen as "reality" while better times are spent with a sense of dread at what disaster is going to happen next. Every time I have a month that does not measure up to my sales goals, I remind myself that at the time of this writing I have had more than 96 months of consistent performance. I'm not reinventing the wheel here. Rather than fret about the future or wonder "Why me?" I simply recommit myself to repeating *tried and true practices*. The details may differ each time, but we all know what works, right? Leverage your Best and Highest Use to find, keep, and grow customers and deliver on what you promised.

As my coach and mentor Alan Weiss says, "The first sale is to yourself." Too many business owners have trouble keeping themselves sold on what they should do. Previous successes are the best antidote to doubt. For example, in my line of work relationships and results are the lifeblood of any successful firm. (Not many business owners look in the Yellow Pages under "Growth Consultant.") Therefore, when my business slows I double my efforts to give my clients and referral sources more referrals, and without fail the more I give, the more I get back. Every now and then, I can still be surprised at how simple this is.

By revisiting your definitions for the three circles of (1) Best and Highest Use; (2) Target Market; and (3) Pain and Opportunity, you can continually refine your efforts to find the right customers and sell them what they need in ways that provide value for them and healthy profits for you. Every time you cycle back through the process, you narrow your focus, eliminating more distractions in order to sharpen your aim.

At this point, when you can see your prospects and customers, your efforts, and the results as if through a telescope, you can start to expand it back out by leveraging the *very best* of all that you do.

Every two years I like to say that I reinvent my business. The truth is I just clarify what I do and how I describe it. Thus, I have evolved from "sales consulting" and "marketing consulting" through "business consulting" into "growth consulting" and my clients are no longer companies of any stripe but business owners. I don't "sell" the tactics of sales and marketing but the results of growth, and my passion lies in partnering with other owners to achieve the growth they and their firms desire and deserve.

At the time of this writing, if you Google "Business Growth Consultant," my *www.andybirol.com* comes up first—not because of my investing in key words, pay per click, or other shortcuts, but because I have published 120 articles on business.

Most recently, I narrowed my focus even further to serve three areas of pain and opportunity experienced by business owners. These areas of service are:

- *Growth acceleration* for thriving companies that strive to do better.
- *Growth through succession or transition* for companies facing leadership changes.
- *Refocusing for growth* for companies with flat or sliding sales and profits.

Because each of these falls within my defined BHU of helping owners grow their companies, they are complementary elements of the same brand, and within each exist tiers of service that allow clients to choose a "little taste of Andy" or "a lot." The system has reduced the time I must spend explaining what I do and who I do it for, because people instantly know whether my services are in line with their needs. The ultimate goal is to repeat patterns of success to grow your business to the next level—at which point the cycle of the five catalysts begins again.

Revisiting the crucial intersection

In Chapter 2 we defined the crucial intersection between your BHU, your target market, and your customer's need as the point at which your firm's capabilities resolve the most customer pain or create the richest opportunities for their business. Because this intersection is highly dependent on what the market needs at any given time, as well as on your company's ability to deliver solutions, you need to reassess it on an ongoing basis. Don't think of it as an intersection of two highways paved into the ground, but as two boat routes that crisscross at irregular points on the water, depending on variables such as motor speed, wind strength, and waves.

Uncovering and predicting customer needs

Sure, they buy from you today, but will your customers still love you tomorrow? What about next year? The only sure thing other than death and taxes is that markets change, technology advances, trends come and go—and businesses that don't adapt go right out of business. In corporate America there is a certain comfort in groupthink and Power Point presentations, but those of us charged with actively meeting the needs of our customers don't have time for distractions and denial. We need a clear vision of where our market is going, how our customers are changing, and how we can translate this knowledge into tangible ways to boost our sales and profits.

Don't obsess about the future and all of its uncertainties, but do acknowledge that it's coming. How can you keep your eye on what customers will want in the future while meeting their needs right now? Here are some guidelines:

- *Embrace your customer base.* Enhance the relationships between your company and your buyers through surveys, Internet newsletters that invite reader response, follow-up calls, on-going service agreements, customer seminars, roundtables, and training sessions— whatever works for you. Some of your company's best ideas may just come from your customers.

- *Keep it real.* Quickly turn what you learn into real–world applications that promote profitable growth. Focus on tangible ways to capitalize on market changes.
- *Enhance your company's Best and Highest Use.* Never abandon what makes you special simply to make some quick cash. While permanent changes in the marketplace may require you to stretch your comfort zone, you need to reconcile changes with your BHU, not trade in one for the other.

Only when you have successfully worked through these steps should you modify or enhance your BHU to deliver more value. Predicting the future is the first step to smart innovation, but your goal is still profitable growth.

Predict customer behavior with events and anniversaries

Where were you when the Challenger space shuttle exploded? Which of your birthdays has been the most special? Most people find the first question easy to answer, as the memory leaps to mind, while the second requires some thought. The Challenger disaster, like JFK's assassination and the terrorist attacks of September 11, 2001, stands alone. These are *events*, one-time occurrences that carve themselves into memory by being strange or special. In contrast, any one of your X number of birthdays is an *anniversary*, a recurring incident that follows an event. Birthdays, wedding anniversaries, or the celebration of religious holidays such as Christmas and Passover are good examples.

Savvy business owners use events and anniversaries to reach their prospects and customers at opportune times. Regardless of what you sell, your business can be broken down into events and anniversaries. You know you are in an *event-driven business* when it takes a random event to provoke customers to buy from your firm. Examples include the window replacement, building construction, and trial lawyer businesses. In these cases, you must market your company to build awareness among the masses of potential customers who might need your products or services some day while serving those customers who happen to need you today. If your customers buy around a predictable, recurring date, however, you are in an *anniversary-driven business*, such as the magazine, insurance, and any service contract industries. These sales go to the company who knows which customers will buy on a given date.

Here are some quick ways to grow your event business:

- Define the event that drives your sale and educate your entire marketplace to look for it.
- Articulate the consequence of the event on your customer's business.
- Link your solution or remedy to the consequence by telling customers how you will eliminate their pain or assure their opportunity.
- Be specific and focus on outcomes. For example, a company that sells replacement windshields might offer trucking companies a priority service plan to get damaged trucks back on the road quickly, reducing their losses.

Marketing an event-driven business is a matter of blanketing the broader marketplace with your company's name and BHU. Capture the attention of 100 percent of your potential prospects—some of them will need you one of these days. Pounce on anyone who signals interest.

To grow your anniversary-driven business:

- Know the exact date, as well as where and how the decision-maker will recommit.
- Know the clients' expectations, sequence for reengagement or disengagement, and trigger events leading up to the repurchase.
- Understand the buyer's experience since the last anniversary and how his or her expectations have changed.

If you are providing brokered health care services, understand how rising health care premiums or employee problems processing medical claims have altered your customer's expectations. If you sell Web hosting services through yearly contracts, determine how your client's Internet business is changing and what upgrades they need by way of search engine, click-through, and hosting rates.

When you market to customers who are anniversary-driven, be extra responsive to satisfaction or dissatisfaction as their commitment date approaches. Don't sell to them the rest of the year, but don't ignore them. Most customers appreciate a few follow-ups to confirm whether their expectations are being met. Also, know what mistakes your competitors make, how they affect your prospects, and exactly what you will do to avoid making them. Then tell your prospects!

Think of how well human beings respond to signals for anniversary and event-driven activities, from renting a tuxedo for a friend's wedding to renewing our driver's licenses. Giving your customers a little training will help you to maximize your results, investment, and returns.

Productizing your services

There comes a time in every professional firm when the need for non–time-based income is compelling, perhaps because of a staff shortage, increased competition from new and lower cost providers, or the desire to offer standardized versions of services to customers at various price points. Many professional service firms can enhance their Best and Highest Use through productizing their services, as long as they recognize that selling products involves more than crinkle bags and gift wrap.

Here are five key questions for service firms that want to productize their Best and Highest Use:

- When is the time to start standardizing?
- What will it take?
- What are the new key success factors?
- What is a reasonable investment in time, effort, and money?
- When are outside resources required?

Classical marketing wisdom states that taking a new product to a new market is about eight times riskier than taking an existing product to an existing market, so you may be better off streamlining the delivery and production of your service before you think about packaging expertise. A better word here is *customization*. Yes, creating tiers of services is a terrific way to adapt to a changing marketplace, but only if you have the resources *and the willingness* to commit to things like 24/7 customer access. Step into the water one toe at a time. Deliver a customized service, produced through a standardized process, for an agreed-upon price.

Growing through adoption

Visit your neighborhood animal shelter and you'll become convinced that just because something has been discarded doesn't mean it lacks value. As the economy shimmies one way and then another, a lot of companies are focusing on fewer products, services, and customers—which leaves quite a few opportunities without a home. So, why not take in another company's cast-off, as long as it fits your BHU? Here are five ways to adopt and grow:

- Ask your customers which products and services their suppliers are ignoring.
- Take your accounts that no longer fit within your company's focus and sell them to other providers.
- Sell your competitors the products and services you are better at delivering.
- Partner with your customers to meet their customers' needs.
- Work with your suppliers to meet the needs of their other customers.

Sometimes, the definitions of trash and treasure depend on who is doing the judging. Or as Paul Simon sings, "One man's ceiling is another man's floor."

Refining: The key to conviction

Did you know that approximately 250 tons of raw ore are mined for every one-carat, gem-quality diamond produced? After digging through layers of soil, miners must cut through kimberlite, or blue rock, to extract rough diamond—not much prettier than its sister product, pencil lead—and subject it to a complicated process of washing, cutting, and refining. Of all the diamonds mined in a given year, less than 20 percent are pure enough to be used in jewelry.

Focusing your company around Best and Highest Use is like finding a treasure map, it's the start of something really good—but it's just the start. Keep digging. Commit yourself to each step of the process. By systematically refining your efforts, you will create that rarest of natural elements: your unique business brand. This involves expanding, enhancing, and growing all the work we have already done.

☑ Self-check: Focused or fuzzy?

Sometimes owners who think their companies are on track are victims of wishful thinking, myopia, or plain old denial. If you are not getting the results you want and think you deserve, you need to reassess. Follow these steps to find out whether your business is really in focus:

- ☐ Show your brochure to a prospect and note his or her reactions. If the prospect seems puzzled, explain the brochure step by step to describe what your company does and how you can help. If he or she still looks puzzled, beware!

- ☐ While visiting clients, call up your company's Website and ask what they think. If they find it confusing, show the site to any teenager you know, and see if he or she loves it.

- ☐ Promise your executives or most valued employees that they will be well compensated and talk up the beauty of Hawaii as you hand out their bonuses. Then call your company's travel agent. How many of them booked two nights at an Econo-lodge in Branson (and can't afford to take the kids)?

- ☐ Grant a long, detailed interview to a business reporter from a local newspaper. When the paper comes out, read the article to see whether the reporter gained any idea of what your firm does.

- ☐ Write down the names and companies of your 10 hottest prospects and show the list to all of your friends. Take note if anyone knows one or more of the prospects and ask why he or she never thought to refer you.

☐ Call up some customers and describe all the new features your firm offers—things your competitors do not do. If they barely react, you know they have no idea how you are distinct from others in your field.

☐ While networking before a business luncheon, count how many different ways you answer the question, "What does your firm do?" Decide how much you sound like a politician moving from one special interest fundraiser to the next.

☐ Ask your employees to describe your business. Then count the ways they choose to do so.

☐ Separately ask your sales force what they are selling and your customers what they are buying. If the answers are different, you need to address whether or not your firm is truly providing the solutions your clients need.

If any of these scenarios is familiar, your firm may be fuzzier than focused. Enlist your staff and work through the PACER Process until everyone sees your company in sharp relief.

Section II

The Milestones of Business Growth

Think of it as a rite of passage right up there on the fun level with spelling bees, bouquet tosses, and wisdom teeth extractions. As soon as your firm shows signs of prospering, The Question—a grown-up version of the exasperating *What do you want to be when you grow up?*—starts coming at you from everywhere. Whether phrased by family members, friends, vendors, staff, or others inside or outside your company, it will sound something like this: "Your business is taking off? Really? So, what are you going to do to make it grow bigger/faster/stronger/more profitably?"

Can't they let you catch your breath? Prepare yourself, because you will be asked a version of this inquiry at each stage of business growth. Most people are well intentioned, but the collective impact of these questions is felt as a subtle pressure to perform up to expectations. Whose expectations? The only good answer is "Yours."

Just as some people don't really want to get married or have kids, some business owners don't really want to grow their companies. They may like the control a small business gives them and feel content with their lifestyle. Perhaps they just aren't willing to invest the resources needed for growth. Choosing to stay small is, for some owners, a viable choice.

We discussed the five catalysts that guide business growth in the first section of this book. Now we are ready to address the issues business owners face at each stage of their company's progress and longevity. The next four chapters examine how companies manage these catalysts through four major sales junctures:

- From $0 to $1 million.
- From $1 million to $5 million.
- From $5 million to $20 million.
- From $20 million to $50 million.

No matter where your business is now, in order for it to grow to the next level you must overcome some common challenges. Knowing where you are, how you got there, and what to expect at each level will help you to anticipate and accomplish what needs to be done. Each level is dominated by one or more catalysts. For example, firms that are starting from $0 or bring in revenues of less than $1 million should apply the majority of their (limited) resources to the first two catalysts, conviction and Best and Highest Use. The sales funnels, delivery systems, and consistency and repetition ideas are also important, but the smallest of small businesses need conviction and Best and Highest Use to build a foundation for sustained growth.

At each successive level, you need to measure your commitment to continued growth. Even the most passionate owners grow old and/or tired, so at some point we all must decide when enough is enough. (Think Steve Jobs leaving Apple to form Pixar, then returning to save Apple.) Sometimes a family business outgrows the family's desire to run it. A common choice here is to sell off one or more divisions, letting the family focus on a smaller core business.

The somewhat derogatory term "lifestyle business" is often applied to owners who prioritize their personal comfort and hard-earned gains over business growth. This strikes me as being unfair. If an owner decides to sell his company based on an honest appraisal of his own limitations, isn't he doing the business a favor? This is fairly common among businesses below $20 million in sales, which make up the majority of all companies on the planet. Why dismiss so many conscientious owners with a derisive label? A true owner knows that his or her business *is* a lifestyle. Therefore, the next four chapters will explore not only what the owner can do to grow his or her business, but also define under what conditions and for which owners growth is not the best option. By clarifying these personal and business choices, owners can make better decisions and execute them accordingly.

The book's final chapter examines the critical process of succession and transition. Handing over the reins of your company may seem like a land far, far away, but in essence, every step a business owner takes is ultimately a step closer to some form of succession or transition. Each chapter ends with a brief "quiz" to measure your company's progress, and in the appendix located at the back of the book, you will find additional exercises for each topic. Be sure to work through the examples carefully, because as you write you might discover or realize things about the way you conduct business that is affecting your ability to capitalize on your growth.

Throughout the book, you will be reminded to stay focused on who you are, what makes your firm special, and where you want to go. Owners who attempt to create mini-versions of the giants in their industries, or of the corporations for which they used to work, rarely succeed to the level of (or have as much fun as) those who assimilate all that they are and wish to become into the core values of the business. When you see your business this way, the horizon expands. You will see the potential to change your firm. I continue to marvel at how my business and my clients' businesses keep racing into new territory as we learn to drive better, enjoy it more, and create more value to delight, excite, and ignite our customers.

Don't forget! When you see this icon, turn to the Appendix for an exercise to help you grow your business.

Because you are reading this book, you probably want to find new customers, keep existing customers, and grow your firm. These next five chapters will present a clear picture of where you are, what brought you to this point, where you want to go, and how to get there. All of this information is rooted in the successes and failures of *real* companies, the product of my analysis of more than 150 of my 300 past and current clients. (Only successes are mentioned by name, of course.) What do these growing firms have in common? What makes a company just average? What factors contribute to a company's decline? My time in the trenches of the real world has allowed me to draw some firm conclusions about business. I encourage you to read on, and discover how to experience seven figure growth!

Chapter 6

The First Day of the Rest of Your Life: Growing from start-up to $1 million

In 1938 (at the age of three) Ron Popeil was shunted off to boarding school after his parents divorced, and lived there for four years, when he and his brother went to live with their grandparents. The family was poor, and Ron's grandfather was a bitter man incapable of providing the affection the boys desperately needed. At the age of 16, Ron went to live in Chicago with his father, a small-time inventor, and took to sales the way a Pocket Fisherman takes to water.

Emboldened by his determination to escape the loneliness and poverty of his childhood, Ron began selling his dad's inventions door-to-door and giving live demonstrations at Woolworth's flagship store. During the summers, he traveled and sold wares at state and county fairs.

By 1964, the year before he turned 30, Popeil was running a company with sales in excess of $200,000. By 1968, following a string of successful products such as the Chop-O-Matic, the Mince-O-Matic, the Veg-O-Matic, and the Dial-O-Matic, Ron Popeil's two-minute, unscripted, demonstration-style commercials were a ubiquitous presence on television, and his company, Ronco, was earning revenues of $8.8 million.

A quintessential American success story, Ron Popeil's rise to fame and fortune shows the power of conviction. Through a combination of natural skills, a shrewd understanding of the marketplace, and good timing, he propelled his Best and Highest Use of connecting directly with customers through the fledgling medium of television, which, by simulating one-on-one communication, took his "live demonstrations" of quirky products into millions of living rooms. Yet, long before he had a product to sell, and before he had ever heard of TV, Ron Popeil was driven by the desire to build himself a better life. His conviction transformed him from abandoned child to a multi-millionaire who is among the 20th Century's most influential entrepreneurs. How many other business owners have a museum in their honor?

Keys to your future

The smallest of small companies (those with annual sales of less than $1 million) can perpetually live hand-to-mouth, on wing-and-a-prayer operations, or they can follow Ronco's example and become nimble firms with great gross margins and healthy futures. What distinguishes a small business that merely scrapes by (or goes out of business) from one that first stabilizes and keeps growing? While all five of the catalysts are important at every stage of a business' life, *conviction* and *Best and Highest Use* are most imperative for new and very small companies.

You may remember from earlier chapters that conviction sets the stage for an owner to identify his or her BHU and deliver it to the most accessible and qualified prospects in a way that resolves their most immediate and acute pain or provides deeply needed opportunity. If the business owner is selling something unique (not a commodity) for which there are many prospects, his or her personal conviction and sharpened sense of Best and Highest Use will help in finding, keeping, and growing the firm's initial customers. Without sufficient energy and passion, however, owners will find that sales or marketing efforts fall flat because small and new companies are indistinguishable from their owners. If an owner can't win over a prospect with the sheer power of his confidence and sincere enthusiasm, what slick marketing gimmick can?

Picture Ron Popiel taping his first TV commercial in the mid-1950s. People thought he was crazy for simply showing up in front of the cameras with no script and no real plan for what he was going to say. Today we are well aware of TV as a medium, but in the early days the astonishing power of television lay in its ability to simulate personal communication, as if Bob Hope, Lucille Ball, and Ricky Ricardo were standing in your living room! By demonstrating his Chop-O-Matic "live" on TV, Ron Popiel brought to his audience the same earnest passion, enthusiasm, and spontaneity that had made him a terrific door-to-door salesman. He didn't need to memorize a script because he didn't need to fake his conviction. The guy was genuinely convinced that his product could be a lifesaver for every house in America, and his audience responded to that sincerity.

In contrast, an individual trying to start a company around a product or service that he or she doesn't find exciting will pass that lackluster attitude on to the prospects and (few) customers, eventually eroding their faith, at which point he or she may be desperately faking confidence like a used car salesman opining the virtues of a 1987 Yugo. Without conviction, no other catalyst even comes into play. Best and Highest Use is the marriage of what you do well with what you love to do, expressed in a way that brings value to a segment of the marketplace. If you feel insecure about the value of what you are selling, or if you are trying to sell something you don't like by doing things you don't love, what's the point?

Zero sum: Starting up

I have started three businesses and only one succeeded. (The one about which I felt, and still feel, the most passion and confidence.) Similarly, I have known many, many individuals who want to start businesses and possess the talents to succeed, yet very few who have turned their potential into stable, profitable ventures. To understand this, take a look at the diet industry: Atkins, Ornish, Weight Watchers, Jenny Craig, Nutri-whatever, and many more. Did you know that the industry rakes in about $50 billion in annual sales—*in a country that keeps getting fatter*? These companies soar to ever greater heights because most people who join a weight loss club, buy a diet book, or stock up on Slim-Fast will either never start their program or quit soon after. Their health is still marginal, they are still overweight, and their spouse keeps complaining about all that cash down the drain, but sticking to a diet program requires a deep sense of conviction that most people simply don't have. (It doesn't help that there's a donut store every two blocks either.)

Business books are the South Beach Diet of publishing—trendy, attractive, exciting, but, for most people, not worth forsaking their next hot fudge sundae. Books about how to start your own company sell like crazy these days. A lot of workers feel disenfranchised, and the American Dream is right there for the taking. Yet, the vast majority of people who buy these books never take the plunge, or they blunder into something they don't really want to do out of a desperate desire to escape. Multi-level marketing companies, which promise to make business owners out of anyone willing to fork over some cash, succeed by appealing to this popular yearning to flip off the boss, sleep late, and get rich in the afternoons. But guess what? The industry has an attrition rate of around 90 percent *in the first three months.*

Contrast this to people who start businesses out of a wellspring of conviction and a desire to serve customers. Their rock-solid belief in what they are doing underlies all of their daily activities and refreshes them during times of disappointment and struggle. These nascent owners have a defining point that fires their determination to succeed and the skills to back it up. So, how do you know you are ready to start your own business? To get from $0 to $1 million in sales means making do with what you have, and typically this doesn't involve bags of money. Here is what you *do* need:

- An idea for a product or service.
- The ability to make it or provide it.
- The passion to sell it.
- Some prospective customers who will buy it in the first 90 days.
- At least three months of living expenses in the bank.
- The drive to push your BHU onto customers, investors, referrers, vendors, and employees, if any.

Notice that each of these factors is about conviction, Best and Highest Use, or a combination of the two. Because the failure rate for new businesses is so high, particularly within the first three years, it's essential to be honest with yourself.

Here are a few more tough issues a service firm needs to face:

- *In terms of product development*, because the partners of a professional firm are the products, their performance and activities must be assessed, packaged, and managed.
- *In terms of pricing*, many service firms still charge by the hour, which allows those with a higher pedigree (Esq., CPA, CFA, MBA, CMC, and so on) to bill at steeper rates. This is convenient for the firm, but not for customers, who buy solutions rather than "hours."
- *In terms of distribution*, how cost effective is it to deliver the actual work product through human means? Are referrals the best way to grow clients, and if so, how can a firm get more of them? And what about the Internet?

Despite the popular perception that professional services cannot be marketed and sold in a quantifiable and measurable manner, it's possible to do it right. Here are some key steps:

- Agree that marketing must become one of the firm's core competencies.
- Hire a marketing expert. No matter how many advanced degrees you have, she knows more about this than you do. And objectivity is essential. Don't hold marketing hostage to disagreements between partners!
- Invest in the Internet beyond a simple Website. It is changing the way professional services are delivered and marketed.

Finally, if you or your partners have misty memories of the time when excellence was measured by your own profession, get over it. Marketing your business is as essential as marketing your firm.

Small but stable

Why do so many small businesses fail in their first five years? While a lack of cash is cited as the primary reason small businesses fail, it often isn't accurate. If you begin a new venture with several months of work lined up, you'll be fine for awhile, and as long as you deliver on what you sell, you will earn repeat business and perhaps some referrals. Just don't confuse this (relatively) smooth sailing with reality.

If your dream is to get big, you've got to start small. In other words, small companies prevail by finding just a few things that some easily accessible customers will buy quickly, probably more because of the owner's enthusiasm than for the "perfection" of the product. Upon securing these early customers, small businesses should invest only the bare minimum of time, money, and effort to make their products and services more attractive to more people. Only in the movies is it true that "if you build it, they will come." When owners of small companies lament that they can't find interested investors or sympathetic bankers, they are probably covering up their own inability to close customers. Even if they stumbled across a pot of gold at the end of a rainbow, the cash influx could compensate for this deficiency only temporarily

The business owner who is able to find a few customers who can pay for some easily delivered version of the company's BHU is positioning his young firm for growth. And as we discussed in Chapter 5, consistency in delivering to the customers' expectations is the first, most important step in building a brand. Many owners are too flushed with excitement to rein in their desire to plaster their business name all over Broadway, but with revenues under $1 million, no company can afford expensive marketing. Time is better spent developing and refining internal systems for finding, keeping, and growing customers, and delivering value profitably. Show me an owner who realizes the importance of making a product or delivering a service that is as good as the hottest prospect or the neediest customer wants it to be, and I'll show you a future star.

If your business is no longer wet behind the ears, but is still earning revenues under $1 million, what do you need to do to succeed at this level?

- Get real customers with real money and real problems to buy your real products or services.
- Keep making, selling, and delivering your BHU to meet customer expectations.

- Analyze your financials to make sure you are delivering profit to your firm along with value to your customers.
- Strike a balance between selling, delivering, and developing. Keep your sales funnel full!
- Put back some of your profits to add to your emergency fund until you have saved the equivalent of six months of expenses. This may feel like hedging your bets, but conviction doesn't require homelessness.

At this stage, your company is probably similar to a toddler: small but energetic, a constant source of amazement to you, who birthed it out of thin air. Many firms of this size also go through a phase similar to the Terrible Twos, when ambition outstrips ability. Once you get past the initial scramble for survival and have a healthy group of customers, you can turn your attention to the new challenges of administration, cost efficiency, and maintaining service. Your goal is to develop reliable systems to manage and assess the effectiveness of each major business activity, from customer relations to cutting payroll. In other words, it's time to put the "business" in your business! Just don't let your efforts interfere with your primary concern of delivering your BHU profitably to customers.

Growing to the next level

Okay, you're in the groove. Customers are content, profits are healthy, and you are starting to think about taking the next step. As your firm nears that magical million dollar milestone, you need to slow down long enough to answer this critical question: *Do you want your firm to grow?*

When the answer is "No"

For many owners—perhaps even the majority—growth is not their goal. They are happy with the way things are. They earn enough money to live at the level they desire. They are managing the challenges of a very small business with aplomb, and they are probably scared to death of what may happen if it gets any bigger. Growing a company takes plenty of time and money, and the bigger it gets, the less control you will have over it.

(Think: child—college—dorm life) If you don't really want to be a superstar, growing to the next level may not be worth it.

If you choose not to grow, you need to concentrate on keeping the business healthy and vibrant. The mindset here is more immediate gratification than building for the future, as your business exists to facilitate your lifestyle rather than the other way around. Your goal is to maximize

Birol's bit: Marketing your professional services firm

Marketing can be a challenge for service providers—accountants, attorneys, consultants, and the like—because the fruits of their labor are intangible. Imagine a psychiatrist running a half-page newspaper ad that features a shrunken head. See what I mean?

Creativity aside, most professional service firms turn to promotional efforts such as seminars, public relations, and image advertising, although the latter can be especially difficult. How does one reliable accounting firm image itself separately from all other reliable accounting firms? These efforts, however, are promotional and should not be confused with actual marketing. Many firms would do better to use other ingredients from the marketing mix0, specifically target marketing, product development, and pricing and distribution. These areas strike at the heart of a business, which is one reason so many firms avoid them. For example, most service firms grow through relationships. By taking a hard look at customers and the cost-revenue ratio they provide, a firm may be forced to admit some relationships are unprofitable. Target marketing requires a more objective selection of clients and customers.

current revenues and profits rather than create value to sell "some day." Invest in knowledge and personal services to make the most of the customers you have and those you can get in the near future. You may remain in the "eat what you kill" mode, but the trade-off comes in having total flexibility and control. Most importantly, if you try to grow when you don't really want to, ambivalence will make sure you get your wish.

When the answer is "Yes, but..."

Some small businesses are simply not ready to grow. They have survived, and their owners are ambitious, but an honest appraisal reveals a company in decline. You know you are in this situation when old customers are leaving you faster than new ones are signing up. Your costs are soaring. You have some long-term fixes in mind, but you don't know whether you can implement them fast enough.

What can you do when your company's back is up against the wall? Put growth aside for now; it's time to perform triage. Here is a quick plan:

- Confirm your basic BHU, target market, and the pain you resolve and opportunity you create for them and decide what, among all options, is most likely to work and easiest to do.
- Determine what you can spend on the business without risking your entire net worth.
- Give your best customers a seat on the lifeboat and do everything you can to service their accounts. Save only those you can make money on *now*.
- Determine three month objectives, activities, and accountabilities for your surviving staff.
- Communicate your plan to banks, staff, customers, and if necessary, the media.
- Build a timetable to roll out your strategy and stick to it.
- Drive forward with a sense of urgency. Your business can bounce back only on the strength of your conviction.

As Jim Morrison sang, "I have been down so long that it looks like up to me!" You may need to take drastic steps to save your business, but you probably won't make things worse.

When the answer is "How soon can I get there?"

If your business is healthy and you are committed to growth, what must you do to reach the next milestone?

- Develop enough capability, momentum, and cushion to reinvest in the business.
- Expand and systematize your sales efforts so that they are predictable and profitable but not all-consuming.
- Get a credit line if you don't have one, or get a bigger one if you do. Decide how much money you need to invest in the business, and use it wisely.
- Actively recruit a group of champions and advocates. These are people who will happily refer your firm because they "get" what you do.

Show me the money

Your company is small. You have identified a need among your customers that the marketplace currently ignores. You have devised a specific plan to offer a new product line to fill this gap. You have spoken with several of your customers who are enthusiastic about your idea. The bad news? You need capital to get it going. No bank or professional lender shares this enthusiasm. In fact, still stung from the dot-com explosion, they are being downright stingy!

What you really think you need is more money from an angel willing to swoop down and help the cash-starved like you. In return for a cash outlay, your angel gets to own a piece of your business and compound your management woes by having a say in how you run your business. And worse yet, this angel's agenda is to get the money back with interest, while yours is to delight your customers. Do you see the inherent conflict in taking outside money with strings? You would be better off borrowing from Pauly Walnuts of the Sopranos. While he wants and will get his debtors to pay up, he doesn't care what your business does as long as you pay him.

There is a better way. Unless your new endeavor requires you to invest everything before you can make a single sale (as in software or science which needs regulatory industry approval) you can approach your best customers and get them to invest as earlier adopters in your new product or service. Finance your growth with the margins dollars they pay you. If the new service or product you envision is for prospects, configure it into a trial-sized piece that you can market to new customers and finance yourself. Do whatever you can to avoid mortgaging your future cash flow or worse yet, your independence. It is just not worth it, regardless of what the payoff could be.

Investing in your own growth

Blaming the financial community for product failures or business stagnation is easy, but a more productive approach is to screen your plan with the same rigor you would use before sinking your hard-earned cash into someone else's idea. Ask yourself these questions:

- Can my investment pay for itself?
- Will my business deliver?
- How, exactly, will my business do the job?

Be specific. Know which customers will pay you enough so that you can bootstrap the initiative without taking finance. Determine whether you have the people, money, time, and energy sufficient to make it happen and continue to execute it without hurting other aspects of your business. If you have the resources and step-by-step plan to turn the idea into reality, you may be ready to go for it. Otherwise, you need to slow down and examine your plan.

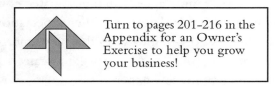

Turn to pages 201–216 in the Appendix for an Owner's Exercise to help you grow your business!

Knowledge industries

Business is all about relationships, especially for small companies, and as an entrepreneur you are likely to get the most positive responses from others who walk in similar shoes. (The element of *quid pro quo* may come into play, so be careful to seek support from and give support only to other owners you respect and trust.) Over the past several years, there has been a lot of speculating about the ways in which business is changing. The knowledge industry is expanding. New professional alliances are displacing many traditional organizations. Technology is making what was once proprietary information more available to those who can really use it. Here are some quick examples:

- Customer knowledge will make or break distributors of all types. From Amway to *amazon.com*, power is shifting and fortunes are being made and lost.
- The nature of alliances is changing. Traditional business organizations, like Kiwanis and Rotary, are working hard to maintain membership levels, while magazines like *Fast Company* and Websites such as *ebay.com* are soaring.
- Technologies, in particular search engines, information portals, and online directories, are making research free to all.

Individually none of these trends are new, but collectively, they are redefining how business can be done. As more suppliers and buyers realize this, a whole new industry will emerge, one that I call "Entrepreneurs eXchanging and Providing Expertise through Relationships and Technology." The great news is that the EXPERT Industry can provide a paved road to your company's next level of growth. The free and fast flow of information has accelerated the pace of business, good news for small companies that tend to be more agile than their bloated competitors. New technologies, new resources, and new customer expectations render many old methods obsolete. Who will survive in this new environment?

- Large companies that manage to gain scale, implement lean solutions, and employ few experts.
- Small to mid-sized companies that specialize and find unique ways to provide expertise to their customers.

While large companies can accomplish their aims through outsourcing and selling to smaller companies, firms in the $0 to $1 million and $1 million to $5 million stages must focus on *gaining expertise* and *building relationships* with knowledge workers, service businesses, customer manufacturers, specialty distributors, and talented freelancers. These goals go hand in hand.

No matter what you currently sell, you need to add expertise to your menu. The "information age" became a cliché only because it is a fact. In terms of expertise, you want to blend content, which is simply your knowledge of products and services, with context, which refers to the unique way you can add value for your customers. Think of it this way: The Internet has turned most forms of content into commodities. How many "mortgage calculators" or actuarial tables can you find on the Internet? Attorneys and consultants offer pieces of their experience, education, and reputations to Web surfers, while a chemical company might post shipping, training, and usage sheets for customers to examine. Anyone with a home page can offer specialty knowledge in exchange for contact information—instant prospecting! One result of this is that "proprietary" content is about as useful as a turntable. Even though we might not like to admit it, vinyl and information ownership are a thing of the past.

How, then, can a small business compete if everyone has the same basic information to offer? You compete by breaking through the information overload. You must understand your niche market. Remember, the more narrowly you can identify the crucial intersection between your offer and their need, the more qualified your prospects will be. While other firms may be able to offer them information, you reach them through *empathy* and *context* by applying your *content* to fulfill their exact needs. A terrific example of the power of context was accomplished by an unlikely source— the U.S. Postal Service—when it began selling stamps through ATM machines. Someone out there knows what it's like to stand in a long line at the post office in December!

You can see that the EXPERT industry is based upon the simple truism that people are social beings. We are all wired to form connections with other people, and we crave relationship when none is forthcoming. In this way, smaller businesses have an advantage at a time when so much in our culture is becoming impersonal and beyond our reach. People want to buy from people. They want to shake hands, exchange information, and build relationships. Therefore, while you can use technology to find qualified experts who can help your business, you should rely on personal connections to close sales. EXPERT relationships happen when others know about you and your business and want to access your expertise, or vice versa. The more you understand about each other's needs and can agree upon and meet each other's expectations, the more you each stand to gain from the relationship.

Turn to pages 215–216 in the Appendix for an Owner's Exercise to help you grow your business!

Client case study: Wittco Standard

While the threat posed by foreign competition on American manufacturers has been well-publicized (and politicized), domestic distributors have been quietly coping with the challenge of the Internet. John Massie, president of Wittco Standard, a family-owned dealer of office and graphic arts equipment, hired me after making the decision to split the original Ohio-based business from the company's larger West Coast operation. The Witt family wanted more control of the regional business, and the break-up was accomplished cleanly, but John Massie found himself running a "new" company from the same old office at a time when his industry was undergoing drastic changes.

Founded in 1960 by John's father-in-law, Wittco started out as an independent office machines dealer selling primarily to the church, school, and print-for-pay markets. The company sold, serviced, stocked, and dealt supplies for a number of manufacturers including Standard Business Systems, MBM, Martin Yale, and Xerox.

Approximately nine years ago, when John stepped into the leadership role, he began transitioning over to solutions selling, and Wittco is now a provider of "finishing systems," basically equipment packages for customers who need to produce their own quality finished documents (church bulletins, educational study guides, company handbooks, and so on) at affordable prices. While the company designs these solutions and services what it sells, more than half of its business is in duplicating machines, small printers that improve on the speed and low cost of copy machines. With the growing popularity of online discount equipment suppliers, Wittco was losing sales. Can a small business really compete with the rest of the planet?

John came to me with a great attitude. He was excited at the freedom he had to grow a small company that was now wholly under his family's control. To start fresh, I took him through the process of identifying and refining two critical issues, Best and Highest Use and target market. Similar to a lot of owners, he couldn't answer the BHU question with much clarity. Then he showed me a stack of letters his company had received from its customers, all of which were full of accolades for Wittco's service technicians. We had found the BHU!

Service-oriented companies provide a very different value to customers than their product-based counterparts, but Wittco was stuck somewhere in between these two categories. While it provided far too much service to be able to slash prices and compete with online dealers, the company was not positioning itself on the basis of its expertise, and it wasn't selling the value of "buying local." As John Massie later commented, "We were providing service above and beyond what we could afford. I came to realize that we were giving an awful lot more than people were paying for, and maybe they would be willing to pay for those services if we asked them."

Because customers aren't created equal, John and I developed a staircase solution, a visual model of five steps of service options from which Wittco's customers can choose. At the bottom is the Internet "drop-ship" model, with prices competitive to online retailers. While Wittco doesn't make much money on those sales, subsequent stairs make up for it, as each step up offers additional value all the way up to a comprehensive package that includes priority service for repairs, discounted supplies, and loaner machines.

The system has had a dramatic impact. For one thing, it absolves the company from providing expensive services and repairs to customers unwilling to pay for them, allowing Wittco to compete with discounters even as it attempts to sell customers the highest service plan that meets their needs. People want to control their own destiny, and they want a clear understanding of what they are getting for their money. And there are enough people who value time over expense and who are willing to pay a premium for the insurance and convenience of a comprehensive service plan.

Wittco is also benefiting in terms of sales strategy. Because higher service levels translate into steeper profits, the company's sales goal is to move customers progressively up the staircase, so we implemented a new commission system that rewards employees for selling higher service packages. We also designed an ordering process that encourages customers to see the value of these extras, such as free delivery and discounted supplies.

According to John, the "hardest part" of this transition was to "internalize the change." He said, "We've had to learn to really listen to [customer] needs and explain the benefits of our plans in ways that apply to them."

It's a new way of doing business, but John and his staff have implemented it beautifully. I showed him the chance to create a niche in the marketplace, and he went for it. Wittco Standard and its customers have benefited greatly from John's conviction and grasp of his company's BHU.

☑   Self-check: How's it growing?

Check your progress through the $0 to $1 million phase of business growth by selecting the answers most applicable to your firm from the following choices:

1.   I have a strong conviction about my company and my products or services. I would describe this conviction as:

a. *Adaptable.* Although I believe my products and services can provide the best value for my target prospects and customers, this doesn't always happen in the ways that I expect. I continue to learn from those who use my products and from those who do not, and I am able to adjust my offer to meet the real needs of my customers.

b. *Stoic.* My products and services are so unique they are only appreciated by people with a high degree of discernment. I make adjustments for no one. Sales aren't as brisk as I'd like, but I am proud of the ones I make and this track record shows me I'm on the right path.

c. *Bipolar.* My belief in my business depends on whether I closed my last prospect or lost another sale. When faced with a new challenge, I typically shut my eyes, take a deep breath, and have faith that everything will work out in the end.

2. In terms of Best and Highest Use:

a. *I Live it.* I used to think of myself as a moonlighter or freelancer, but now I see that I simply was uncertain how to deliver my blend of skills and passion to a slice of the marketplace. I'm not an independent anymore. I run a company and am building my brand.

b. *I know it.* I am aware of my marketplace and can target good prospects and customers. I think I'm ahead of the game, compared to a lot of small companies.

c. *I can skip it.* The whole BHU thing is a little too touchy-feely for me. I'm in this business to make money, period, and I don't have time to spend thinking about what I like to do or do well. As long as people are paying me to work, what's the use?

3. To find, keep, and grow customers, my staff and I:

a. *Hunt with a license.* We have learned how to sell to our target prospects and keep selling to our customers, either through experience or training. We go after new customers aggressively.

    b. *Do okay.* We market to make our competitors envious and our vendors happy. We're on the side of supply; the role of market demand is overrated.

    c. *Hit and miss.* Sure, we make sales but the successes seem random. Why don't more people want to buy from us?

4. Delivering our products and services:
    a. *Is a no-brainer.* My employees and I have a lot of experience in this area, and we deliver on our promises to customers.
    b. *Requires a lot of work.* We are committed to meeting our customer expectations. but unfortunately we end up having to reinvent delivery time after time.
    c. *Just happens.* They buy, we hand the product over. What else is there to think about?

5. As for repetition and consistency:
    a. *We feel challenged.* We haven't mastered this catalyst, but we are working on it.
    b. *We know we need it.* With more experience, we figure it will eventually happen.
    c. *We'll think about it later.* First we need to quite repeating all the same mistakes.

If you circled mostly "a" answers, your company is on its way to the next milestone of growth. A "b" majority indicates that your firm is stable but you need to strengthen your firm's foundation to achieve more profitable growth. A lot of "c" answers? The bad news is that your business is in decline, but the good news is that once you know this, you can start making necessary changes.

Chapter 7

Gaining Traction:
Growing from $1 million to $5 million

Rudy Giuliani's heroic leadership in the days following the September 11th terrorist attacks in New York City has nearly wiped from memory his September 10th status as a scandal-ridden, lame duck politician. He was once the butt of late-night comedians, dogged by bad publicity following a very public infidelity, a very nasty divorce, and a bout with prostate cancer that had seemingly shaken the core of the feisty, confrontational crime-fighter New Yorkers had come to know. But Giuliani's conviction was credited with holding the city together during its darkest hour. He filled the nation's television screens with a gritty resolve, modeling for millions the triumph of endurance over exhaustion, of necessity over pain.

It's easy to forget that Giuliani left office just a few months after September 11th. As business-executive-turned-public servant, Michael Bloomberg assumed the post of Mayor at City Hall, Giuliani traded in politics for instant business success. In January of 2002, along with former NYPD commissioner Bernard Kerik, he founded Giuliani Partners, a consulting firm affiliated with Ernst & Young. Signing clients as diverse as Purdue Pharma, the U.S. Department of Justice, and Nextel, the company soared into the top ranks of consulting firms, becoming what the *New York Times* described in a February 2004 article as "one of the most novel and lucrative ventures ever begun by an out-of-office American politician."

Granted, few new business owners start out as national heroes. Nor do most of us possess a network of high-powered connections extending across the globe. Yet, while Giuliani's reputation was a major factor in the rapid success of his firm, he deserves a lot of credit for knowing who he is, what his market needs, and how he and his staff can deliver results. In other words, Rudy Giuliani leveraged his Best and Highest Use to create one of the country's most prestigious consulting firms specializing in domestic security, and he did it almost overnight.

Key catalysts

The Giuliani example points to some of the most important attributes of companies that have reached the $1 million to $5 million level of growth. Their client list has expanded from a single (large) company to include diverse entities for which the firm provides an array of services leveraging its BHU. Rudy Giuliani, the embodiment of his company's expertise in security and crisis management, travels extensively, speaking to groups, and managing client acquisition and development. His depth of involvement in the actual work of the company may depend upon the client, but his primary role doesn't involve staying chained to a desk!

Think back on how you got your business to this point. You have:

- Developed the capacity to handle multiple challenges.
- Committed yourself to learning how to find, keep, and grow customers.
- Learned to sell your products and services, perhaps mainly on the strength of your conviction and the infectiousness of your enthusiasm.
- Gained the support of other people who share your vision of how to serve your customers and grow your company.

The future growth of Giuliani Partners largely rests on Rudy's choice of legacy and whether to stay in business or return to politics. While you (probably) aren't staying up nights wondering whether to run for President, when your business is at the $1 million to $5 million level you face a similar option: to grow, or not to grow? Your decision will dictate how you should apply your BHU to find, keep, and grow customers.

As your firm grows beyond the ranks of the smallest of small businesses, with sales in excess of $1 million, it's only natural to experience some growing pains. Along with the joy you feel at your company's success may come the realization that your baby is becoming less dependent on you. Whether you began as a sole proprietor or with a staff of 10, as an entrepreneur you were your firm's chief salesperson, promoter, organizer, and message to the marketplace, but as the company grows in size and complexity, you won't have enough hours in the day to oversee business functions. Many owners have a hard time "letting go" even a little bit, but remember that increasing sales indicate you are doing a lot of things right! The question is, are you satisfied with your business the way it is? Would you be content to keep sales around their current level in exchange for retaining more control over your company? Or are you hungry for bigger numbers, greater prestige, and the chance to create a legacy?

Turn to pages 216–230 in the Appendix for an Owner's Exercise to help you grow your business!

Succeeding at this level

While we all want to do well, success can be risky. If you have grown your business from nothing, achieving sales in the $1 million to $5 million range is cause for celebration—but not for complacency. Smart owners at any level not only guard against backsliding, but also position their firms to ride future waves of opportunity, whether their goal is to stay afloat or cross to the other side of the sea. To do well at this level, you will need to do the following:

- Systematize sales and delivery in order to achieve some level of predictable, positive outcomes.
- Generate results through others in one or more areas.
- Depend less on a few customers, staff, and vendors and reach out to new ones.
- Drive profits and growth by establishing a cost-effective, customer-centric service component to what you are selling.
- Figure out how to consistently produce to a standard, even if you don't yet know how to scale it up.
- Buckle down a signature product in a single market as the foundation for future expansion.

My friend and client John Bukovnik is a great example of how owners can adapt their businesses (and themselves) to new levels of growth. John's company, Easy2 Technologies, rocketed to success nearly as quickly as Rudy Giuliani's consulting firm, and without the national press coverage. He and Paul Schutt founded their company in January of 2000 with the intent to produce home improvement content on their own Website, a business model that sounded better in the latter days of the Internet boom. Within a few months, the stock market sagged, technology and dot-com firms were suddenly suspect, and the flood of venture capital dried up seemingly overnight. Add to this the high cost of advertising and the low traffic flow to the Easy2 Website and not many people would have second-guessed a decision to shut down the baby business.

Instead, John revised his plan to fit the realities of the marketplace. Less than a year after starting the company, he began producing home improvement tutorials and computerized demonstrations for other vendors to host on their sites. This time, the market took notice. John soon signed a deal with a national home improvement retailer, a big box powerhouse that became both a customer and a business partner to the young firm. Hired to develop animated, interactive product demonstrations, tutorials, and buying guides for shoppers to access through the retailer's Website and in many of its 1,100 stores, Easy2 also gained business from many of the superstore's vendors, including national brands like Möen and ClosetMaid. The company wasn't yet two years old. Not long after taking its first steps, this toddler had qualified to run in the Olympics!

A few months later, John gave me a call. There was, as he later said, nothing "terribly wrong" with the company; he simply wanted to get his "compass settings" for the next phase of growth. What a fantastic opportunity for a growth consultant. While a lot of owners wait to get help until they're really in trouble, John recognized that even good companies have vulnerabilities. The sooner they get addressed, the greater the company can become.

I spent a lot of time talking with people at the company to see how things got done and what their perceptions were, and I visited many of the firm's top customers. The product line was terrific, but there was a soft spot in client services. A single executive had been managing both business development and client relations, a valiant effort but an increasingly unrealistic task considering the company's explosive growth. *Finding customers* was easy; new business was flowing in fast with no end in sight, taking attention away from existing customers.

Easy2 needed to focus on *keeping* and *growing* the customers it already had, or risk losing business down the road. John created a new position, director of client services, and brought in fresh talent to cultivate buyers into loyal customers. We restructured the sales process to streamline approval of new projects and allow the firm to manage large, complex orders, and developed new systems and scheduling tools to handle ten-fold increases in orders.

In focusing on the firm's BHU, John and I identified some untapped opportunities. Easy2 provided excellent technical and feature functionality, but its customers wanted more information about how their buyers adapted and used the products. By examining the products from the end-user's perspective, John and his staff discovered related needs, designed new solutions, and bundled products and services. This was a classic win–win. The company increased customer loyalty, simultaneously boosting its own profits. In the first year after I worked with John Bukovnik, Easy2 Technologies enjoyed a 75 percent increase in sales and is still growing. Easy2 Technologies is no longer the hot young upstart. Instead, as John noted, it is "one of the most advanced companies in [its] field." In fact, it has refined its BHU into the most formalized, comprehensive program for finding, keeping, and growing customers among its competitors.

Birol's bit: Who's selling your stuff?

One question that plagues many business owners involves whether to entrust their sales to an inside staff or hand over the goods to outside reps. While small companies should focus first on their Best and Highest Use and outsource everything else, this doesn't always apply to selling products and services. As an owner, you are also employee number one and, therefore, you are probably your firm's top salesperson. But as a firm grows, the owner can't make every sale. So, who do you trust to sell your stuff?

This question has become more critical for smaller and mid-sized businesses because of the growing trend of "big box-ization," which eschews outside sales reps in favor of forcing manufacturers to place captive sales staff on-site. If your sales force focuses more on activities and service than on results and sales, or if your independent reps keep demanding more support without delivering better results, you are probably on the wrong track. Here are some tips for knowing when you need "outlaws" and when to hire "inmates":

Consider using manufacturers or outside reps when you need to sell to existing customers immediately, when a sale will be lost if you don't have adequate sales coverage, and when commission is the preferred form of compensation. But build a captive sales staff when your aim is to sell beyond the purchasing agent and reach deeper into the customer's company, including their new product development functions.

Go with the outlaws if your main goal is to grow volume, not build relationships. If you need to open new markets by taking new products to new customers and/or saturate a defined geographic territory, you need a cast of inmates loyal to your firm.

Success through stability

While John Bukovnik has wholeheartedly embraced his firm's potential for growth, not all owners want to follow this model. What if you are happy with the way things are? To bend an old cliché, do you live to work or work to live? If your business is less about creating a legacy or quadrupling sales than about achieving and maintaining a lifestyle while you do what you love doing, you may be happier sticking with the status quo. Growing to the next level requires a lot of sweat equity and investments in money and time, and it will dramatically alter your relationship with your business.

Asking yourself *whether* you want to grow is the first important question. The second involves whether you *can*. Sometimes owners are so central to the performance of their companies that the business simply can't thrive without them. In these cases, the entire firm revolves around one brightly shining star. Is that you?

If the only reason your staff shows up on Monday morning is to earn a paycheck, you don't have the support you need to get to $10-million in sales, or beyond. Deciding to grow under these circumstances would require radical change. It is possible to do so, as we will discuss in the next section, but you need to know what you're up against. Be honest. Is your company meeting its sales goals, or are *you* meeting its sales goals? You know your company is still dependent on your ability to sell if:

- Your best customers won't buy from anyone in your firm but you.
- The sales pros haven't produced big numbers to justify their salaries.
- Your associates continue to come to you to close important deals.

Even if you have dozens of employees, the business may still be all about you. If you prefer it that way, you can stabilize growth by organizing the firm around your proven strengths and chosen activities. Your Best and Highest Use won't just be the foundation for your company's efforts in finding, keeping, and growing customers—it will *be* those efforts.

Here are some key steps to follow if you choose stability over growth:

- Delegate responsibility for production, delivery, administration, lead qualification, and service so that you can concentrate on sales and customer development.

- Train your inside people to understand what constitutes an opportunity or need for your involvement. Delegate everything else (including the actual work) to your staff whenever possible.
- Document your process for qualifying leads and up-selling existing customers. Create the right questions for your staff to ask and hold them accountable for the number and quality of opportunities they generate for you.
- Take your money out whenever it is not immediately helping you deliver more business. Reduce overhead, streamline operations, and run the company for results rather than dreaming of a future fat payout. Selling out is not an option for most owner-focused firms. Because no one can step into your role and grow the company, your business will last as long as you do.

What are the benefits of maintaining rather than growing your business? By staying a $1 million to $5 million firm, you can remain in a single marketplace or product line and pretty much do things the way you want to do them. Unless you are designed to be a corporate manager, this level allows you to stay *you*. Deciding to grow, on the other hand, means giving up the "my way/my world" mindset, but it may be worth it if you have the power, drive, and sheer desire for more.

Growing to the next level

So, what does it take to grow beyond $5 million in sales? You must develop a sharp clarity of purpose which is scalable; commit time and resources to develop a systematic, repetitive sales and marketing process; and polish either sales or delivery while understanding that the other one must be reinvented. Most of all, you need to possess an intense desire to "own" a market niche, a brand, or a category.

I've already stated that your primary task at this level of growth is to hone your Best and Highest Use and drive it through every level of your organization by strengthening your systems for finding, keeping, and growing customers. If you decide to keep your small business small, the link between your BHU and the sales funnels is obvious even at the $1 million to $5 million level.

To sustain future growth, however, you can't keep such a tight grip on the reins. Whereas earlier we discussed how to design your marketing, sales, and customer service efforts around your BHU, now you need to nail in place systems that accomplish the same goals but rely less on your personal involvement. One of these days you're going to have to take a break, whether it's a month-long jaunt to the islands or a three-week stay in the cardiac ward, so you need to start positioning your firm to do well without you. Your baby is growing up, my friend.

Many owners find this loss of control frustrating and frightening. This is why you need to infuse them with a vision of your firm's Best and Highest Use so that they become extensions—albeit with their own unique talents, some of which may surpass your own—of your strategy for finding, keeping, and growing customers. Motivating your staff isn't enough. An unbroken stallion is motivated, after all, and proves it with every rider it throws off into the dust. Instead, you want to get your people invested in your company's success by investing themselves in your company. You need to develop a corporate culture that fosters individual contributions while providing clear direction in terms of what is best for the firm.

Creating a corporate culture

Much has been written about creating a sense of "ownership" among employees so that their self-interest is aligned with the best interest of their employers; thus, the popularity of company stock and profit-sharing as elements of compensation packages. A more fundamental method is simply to communicate with your staff. Without a strong sense of what the company is (and is not) and of what it does (and does not) your employees won't feel a sense of purpose, and they won't know what you would like them to do in a given situation.

As the owner, you are the only person who can define and apply BHU for your company, but you can't do it alone. Your personal strengths, preferences, and goals will determine the boundaries of your business, so your staff needs to understand them. If you haven't already done so, discuss the following areas with your employees:

Developing a system. Improve customer retention and development by creating processes based on the answers to these questions:

- Is your company transaction-based or relationship-based? In other words, do your customers want you to meet their acute needs quickly and efficiently (without "bothering" them too much), or are they looking for a deeper relationship? Do your processes reflect this?
- What will your company be to its customers: Nordstrom's, Target, or Wal-Mart? Find your niche and stick with it. Knowing what customers expect will help you make important decisions regarding quality, price, and customer service.
- What will you do for customers, and what won't you do? Your best customers are out there, so focus on them.
- How can your marketing and customer service efforts reflect the above? Once you and your staff understand your BHU, you need to make everyone else (potential best customers!) understand it, too.

Delivering the goods. Measure, assess, and improve all that your firm does to meet your customers' expectations.

- What part(s) of your business do customers most value?
- Do your costs reflect your value?
- Is your company a customizer or a mass producer? A job shop, continuous processor, or a low-cost producer?

Controlling growth. Assess your people, activities, functions, and programs in terms of how they contribute to the firm's overall growth. Develop initiatives that deepen employee commitment to growth (both their own and the organization's). You may want to consult business advisors to help you create the kind of organization you need.

As you make necessary changes to systems, structure, staff, and salaries, be sure to talk with your employees. You don't have to explain everything, but by showing your staff why the changes are both necessary and positive, you will create a sense of camaraderie. And employees who feel personally invested in the company's success will work harder and smarter.

Encouraging employees to act like owners

The ultimate goal in developing a corporate culture is to get your entire staff to be independent, innovative thinkers able to perform as a team to row your business in the direction of your choosing. Toward this end, it is important to reward results but also recognize sincere effort. As awful as it is to watch an employee screw up, or to clean up the mess afterward, it's even worse to be told, "Well, you didn't tell me I should do that." Someone who does the wrong thing for the right reason won't do as much damage to your firm as someone who does nothing.

Your responsibility is to educate your personnel and correct them when they make mistakes, so don't punish someone for a good effort that nets a not-so-good result. Many people enter the workforce caring deeply about what they do but wind up being apathetic because their sincerity is never acknowledged. If your people give up rather than follow up, take a hard look in the mirror. Would you want to work for you? Better yet, if you ever escaped a corporate job, did your leaving have anything to do with the frustrations of being undervalued or micro-managed?

Get everyone on the same page by nailing down systems for finding, keeping, and growing customers. Turn back to Chapter 3 and make copies of the customer acquisition, retention, and development sales funnels. Give a copy to everyone on staff, or post the funnels around the office to serve as constant reminders of the fundamentals of finding, keeping, and growing customers. Clearly define the goals and activities for each funnel stage. Once your employees understand which activities to perform, when to enact them, and why, you can give them room to succeed. This will give you the freedom to focus on your personal Best and Highest Use to take your company to the next level of growth, and beyond.

Client case study: Integrated Precision Systems

When a business is growing rapidly, the owners don't have much room for trial and error, a real challenge for those who haven't yet learned how to be business owners. In 1998, Jim Butkovic and Greg Ponchak founded Integrated Precision Systems as a friendly "spin off" of their former employer, a provider of security systems. With decades of combined experience, Butkovic, Ponchak, and their five employees delivered high-level solutions such as employee badging and identification cards, network-based access control, and digital closed-circuit camera surveillance, to a booming market of corporations, schools, bureaucrats, and everyone else concerned with protecting their systems, data, employees, and customers as the new millennium approached. Such easy success proved a mixed blessing.

The young firm was so busy handling customers and designing solutions that business development, administrative functions, and marketing plans were left to simmer on the back burners, and Jim and Greg faced a series of real staircase problems. As soon as they reached a new level of growth, they barely had time to catch their breath before another step appeared, rendering "long-term" solutions obsolete.

Worried about losing opportunities, Jim hired me in 1999 to design a direct marketing plan. IPS had no system for finding customers, so we developed a simple process that would maximize customer acquisition while reducing the time needed to find and sign prospects. Within 10 weeks, the campaign surpassed expectations. Six months later, Jim called me to report that the new marketing plan was accounting for more than one-third of the company's total business.

Sales at IPS stayed strong—it's hard to overestimate the potential of the market—but Jim and Greg had no time to implement reliable processes for other crucial areas such as staffing, compensation, and sales coordination. They hired me back to get things moving toward several goals, including launching new products, implementing warranties, service plans, and upgrades, and balancing prospecting with customer development. Jim later commented that while some of what we did was "easy," other changes, such as terminating unnecessary or unproductive personnel, were "tremendously difficult" at the time.

IPS is reaping the rewards today. Since 1999, the company has grown to 19 employees and sales have averaged a 100 percent increase *each year*. The company's innovations include iSolve, an online knowledgebase of more than 12,000 pieces of technical support information, and the Web based EnterpriseID, which allows users to design, create, and purchase ID cards and supplies directly over the Internet. "Business owners need...to view the business from a different perspective and spot potential problems," said Jim Butkovic, "and think long-term....You never know what you'll see."

☑ Self-check: How's it growing?

Check your progress through the $1 million to $5 million phase of business growth by selecting the answers most applicable to your firm from the choices below.

1. At this level, my conviction is:
    a. *Wavering.* If I could find a buyer, I would consider selling the business. Or maybe I should just shut it down. Running this company is harder than I ever expected. Still, once in a while we have some good days.
    b. *Pretty strong.* My company is doing fine, but I'm a realist. I run a small business, so there are a lot of things I just can't do.
    c. *Stronger than ever.* My firm is doing better than I expected, and I can see more good things coming in the future, at least for the next few months.

2. In terms of Best and Highest Use:
    a. *I don't get it.* I'm still waiting for the business market to respond to my offer. Why don't more customers care about what my firm can do?
    b. *I got it.* Been there, done that. Still have the t-shirt.
    c. *I am getting there.* As I learn more about my prospects and customers, I keep seeing new opportunities to serve them. I can also tell when a prospect isn't a good fit with my business, and I can't waste time trying to twist my firm into knots just to make a sale.

3. To find, keep, and grow customers, my staff and I:
    a. *Are consistent.* We keep trying, and we keep failing. Three facts of life: death, taxes, and prospects not returning our calls.

    b. *Are focused.* When we concentrate on finding customers, we really do a good job, but then we start having trouble holding on to our existing buyers. If we focus on keeping customers, however, we don't get enough new business streaming in.

    c. *Work together.* They set up the pins and I knock 'em down. I still close most of our business and maintain customer relationships, but my employees are gaining skills and confidence in sales and service.

4. Delivering our products and services:

    a. *Is more complicated than it used to be.* Customer complaints are up, and we've lost a few accounts.

    b. *Is what it's always been.* I haven't thought much about it, actually.

    c. *Is a work in progress.* We've made some real strides, but current sales are stretching our capacities. We are working on improving our systems.

5. As for repetition and consistency:

    a. *We'll think about it later.* We have enough to do to make it from this month to the next, so this isn't something we've even considered.

    b. *We know we need it.* It's a question for the future. Right now, we are trying to build a track record.

    c. *We feel challenged.* Our company and brand are becoming established. In fact, they are pretty much indistinguishable from one another. The prospect of investing money, time, and energy into building our brand is daunting, but we know we need to do it and are taking small steps.

If you circled mostly "a" answers, your company is declining and you must take action quickly before sales, service, and delivery slip even more. A "b" majority indicates that your firm is stable but you need to make some changes if you want to grow to the next level. A lot of "c" answers? Your firm is poised and energized to keep growing!

Chapter 8

Tasting Confidence:
Growing from $5 million to $20 million

"Work hard. Have fun. Make history." This now-famous mission statement of the giant online retailer *amazon.com* encapsulates the essential catalysts of conviction, Best and Highest Use, and sales and delivery (in a slightly different order). Amazon founder Jeff Bezos, who wrote the company's business plan on his laptop computer in an old Chevy driven cross-country by his wife, saw his chance to "make history" in 1994 when he quit his job on Wall Street after learning that the Internet (whatever that was) was growing at an astonishing annual rate of 2300 percent. Thus was born "Earth's Biggest Bookstore," operating out of the garage of Bezos' newly rented home in Seattle.

For Bezos, the passion was less about selling books than about seizing the opportunity to reinvent the wheel—or, at least, the way people shop. In 1995, fewer than 15 million people worldwide had regular online access, but Bezos built his company to showcase the power of E-commerce. Books were easy to pack and ship, the major market players (Barnes & Noble and Borders) represented less than 15 percent of the market, and customers interested in trying out a new point-and-click purchasing method didn't have to worry about choosing the right size, style, or other customized product feature. In addition, most of the people already on the Internet—those with a computer, a modem, and the ability to use them—were college-educated and had high levels of disposable income, two common characteristics of the book-buying market. Amazon went online in July 1995. Three years later, Jeff Bezos' goofy grin was on the cover of *Business Week*, and in 1999, he was named *Time* magazine's "Person of the Year."

Is this a simple example of "right place, right time" success? The gestalt theory is part of it, but to understand why Amazon avoided the great flameout of other virtual companies we need to consider the effect of delivery. I'm not just talking about shipping books. In 1995, most of us were Internet virgins. What made Amazon special wasn't just the cool convenience of shopping in our bathrobes—a lot of companies were offering that—but how gently and efficiently it coaxed us through those thrilling, daunting, early experiences online.

This is conviction, Best and Highest Use, and sales all wrapped up and delivered right in the buyer's lap, a terrific model for owners of any size company, but especially pertinent for those whose firms are growing out of the small business category and into middle markets. Amazon's customer-centric focus led it into a different direction from many other E-commerce companies. Instead of dazzling people with technology—animated graphics were amazing, but who had time to wait for a flashy home page to load over a 28K modem? Amazon prized simplicity by translating its technical capabilities into an easy-to-use search and buy experience (from the customer's side) and into extremely efficient systems for pick, pack, and ship (from the company's side). Rather than pouring money into Super Bowl ad time, Jeff Bezos focused on meeting customer needs for convenience, speed, and reliability. Customer loyalty and word-of-mouth have kept it growing from the virtual company that couldn't make a profit (until 2002) into a sales powerhouse with 2004 annual sales surpassing $8 billion and profits approaching $600 million.

Moving on, moving up

With revenues in that range, Amazon has passed through this level of growth many times over, yet it remains a good example of what it takes for companies to get here. Not so long ago, Amazon enjoyed enormous sales but zero profits, and critics labeled it an emperor with no clothes. How did it cover the enormous costs and become profitable? By doing all the things you've been doing to reach the $5 million to $20 million level of growth:

- Making recurrence an important company goal.
- Understanding that while you can't always change demand, you can co-opt and exploit what customers believe they need.
- Taking chances and risking what you have achieved, even if you make mistakes, in order to reach higher.
- Effectively delivering to your customers and implementing a systematic approach to all phases of your business.
- Staying passionate about delivering value to your customers.

To succeed at this level, you need to strengthen your efforts at recurrence by developing sales and marketing programs to further exploit your opportunities, and you may need to expand beyond the single product/single market identity. Be tough. Whatever the bottlenecks in the company—and there are some—deal with them now. You may need to be ruthlessly selfless. For example, if a pet business, product, or executive is draining the company's resources or efficiency, what must you do? As every triage doctor in an ER knows, some people must be treated now, some later, and others not at all.

The point here is that it is no longer all about you—it is all about the *company*. The business is growing an identity and purpose distinct from your own.

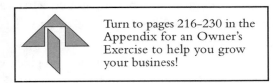

Turn to pages 216–230 in the Appendix for an Owner's Exercise to help you grow your business!

Promise-keeping for profit

Your perception of the value your company delivers matters less than what your customers believe. Yet, your customers' perception of the value they are getting won't matter at all if your company can't turn a profit. To succeed, delivery has to work for everyone.

As you scale up to meet increased sales, keep your eye on these three crucial aspects of delivery and fulfillment:

- The customer expectations you set and meet.
- The impact (real value) of your service on your customers' results.
- Your firm's true cost and opportunity cost of meeting expectations and delivering real value to your customers.

Companies can mess up delivery in three ways: by delivering too little, by delivering too much, or by delivering all the wrong things. By balancing customer expectations, real value, and your costs—and pricing right—you can avoid these mistakes.

Sell and price your value

In contrast, what do you think of when you hear "UPS"? Dependable, right? Reliable. Plain. *Brown*. When you can sum up a company's philosophy in a single color, that's a successful brand! UPS has earned a virtual copyright on the color brown by creatively marketing its own dullness as a symbol of the company's consistency. Hey, when you ship product, whether it's an order of 10,000 widgets, or a birthday gift for your mom, you're not paying for flashy trucks or delivery with a song. You just want it there on time. Have you seen the TV commercial featuring a local "weatherman" struggling against hurricane-strength winds, warning viewers that the city had shut down because of a raging storm as a UPS delivery man quietly loads his (brown) truck in the background? This isn't just cute marketing. UPS knows what its customers want, is selling the value of its reliability, and reliably delivers on the promise.

The plain brown box image of UPS exposes a glaring vulnerability of the U.S. Postal Service (less reliable) and a potential liability of a flashier competitor, FedEx (more expensive). In terms of shipping speed, UPS is in the middle, and its price reflects this. As owners anxious to avoid alienating our customers, we sometimes forget that the way we price our products and services sets an expectation in the minds of customers. Proper pricing, which by definition balances sales volume against net profit, is a crucial element of delivery.

Pull out your latest data and crunch the numbers to see how your firm's current prices are related to net profits, market share, and customer retention rates. To help you make sense of the figures, here are some important guidelines:

Rule 1: Sell the value they are buying

Prospects and customers need to feel comfortable with what they are buying, whether it's a Cabriolet or a year's worth of accounting services. Features, benefits, and capabilities are fine, but sell customers on outcomes. Understand their business objectives and explain the ways your products and services either resolve pain or create opportunities for them. Create an image in their mind, and they'll focus more on outcome than price.

Rule 2: Cover your opportunity cost

This goes beyond just what it costs to make a widget. Your energy, education, and the opportunity cost—what you could be doing with your time and money elsewhere—must be factored in. Sure, you can discount to develop a customer or sign a marquee client, but you and the customer should agree on just what you are getting in return. A big-name client may act as a reference for your firm, but make sure he *agrees* to do it before slashing your margin to gain his business.

Rule 3: Differentiate transactions from relationship sales

Your business is primarily transactional when you must continually re-sell your offer, even to customers who have purchased from you in the past. Your business is relationship-oriented when loyalty is important to you and to your customers.

If your business is transactional, loyalty simply does not drive customer behavior in your market, so you need to price every sale in order to make a profit. On the other hand, relationship selling gives you more flexibility because your compensation is stretched over the life of the relationship. You might lower your cost initially to gain new customers, then increase your prices (and margins) as their reliance on your company grows.

Rule 4: Differentiate events from anniversaries

Remember that an event sale has no guarantee of being repeated, so your price must cover all your costs and provide enough profit, per transaction, to sustain your business. If you price simply to break even, you will end up breaking your business. An anniversary sale will be repeated at predictable intervals, so concentrate on meeting your customers' expectations consistently so that repeat purchases are "no-brainers." Because customers save time *not* looking around for another supplier, your price should reflect that value.

Rule 5: Don't forget warranties and service agreements

Warranties and service agreements accomplish two important goals for your business. First, they provide a degree of comfort for customers. Second, they can immunize your company against unreasonable customer demand while growing your profit margins, but only if you price them correctly.

A properly priced warranty will reassure customers while covering your typical cost to provide those services. Figure out what a product or service typically requires in "after-sale attention" and compare this to the typical customer's need and ability to pay. For example, a supplier of high-end medical equipment to doctors in private practice might offer annual service plans covering monthly checks and maintenance. Because the supplier knows most problems can be avoided through maintenance, he lowers his risk of having to replace components under warranty, keeps his customers satisfied, and earns that monthly service fee.

Price your agreements and warranties to encourage customer behavior to match your perfect model. If the customer is high maintenance, set a high deductible or price-per-occurrence. On the other hand, if the customer's concern is higher than what they will probably need, consider offering unlimited service for a fixed price.

Rule 6: Know the limits of what pricing can do

Remember that if your products and services are inelastic, slashing prices won't change customer behavior in significant ways. Price is sometimes more important to you than it is to customers. Don't price yourself out of the market—but don't give away your Best and Highest Use, either.

Consider the cost

Many entrepreneurs believe they can't be choosy when it comes to customers when, in fact, they can't afford not to be. Sagging margins have one remedy: prioritizing profits over sales volume.

Many companies decide to sell to a group of customers or prospects based on an analysis of the "S" of SG&A (sales, general, and administrative) on a company's P&L statement, yet the direct costs of creating a product or service may differ widely among customer segments. Rather than deciding to "go" or "no-go" solely on the project's cost of sales, we need to uncover the hidden cost data, which may be affected by marketplace, customer needs, or usage. Customers who cost more than they return to your company are expendable.

Specifically, you can assure that your gross margins are maximized within different customer segments by following these tips:

- Account for the time it takes to create a product or service for key customer segments.
- Distinguish between the costs of creating the first customer order versus repeating the process for ongoing reorders.
- Understand the varying levels of direct overhead (or overtime) that are required by different market segments.
- Identify the differences in returns or rework among major customer groups.

Which pockets of your business contribute to the bottom line? Which are being subsidized by it? All customers are not created equal.

Managing customers from hell

If you've been in business longer than a week, you have met your own version (probably many times over). Here are some of my personal favorites:

- The client who asked me to submit a fake (and higher) bid so that his would win.
- The owner who asked to buy 20 minutes of my time at his place at 5:30 in the morning.
- The entrepreneur who reneged on a commitment before asking me to serve as a reference for him.

Clients from hell aren't born, they are made by those who serve them. *Never* say, "Just tell me what you need and it's done." You think you're offering five inches, but the customer may grab five miles!

The more profligate you become, the less your customers will respect you in the morning, so don't lead them into the temptation of exploiting you or your business. Instead, delight them within boundaries that are appropriate, constructive, and mutually profitable. If that doesn't work, cut bait.

Some customers will test your limits. Be clear as to what you are providing and what you are not, and put key terms in writing. If you choose to over-deliver, explain to the customer why you are making an exception. Customers can't value what they don't understand and usually don't value what they get for free. If a customer asks you to do something that may jeopardize your business or reputation, politely decline. No sale is worth more than who you are and what you stand for. I am always amazed at sales people who can't say no. If your customer asks for something outside of your BHU and it is not something you should learn to do, your business can't afford the distraction.

Here are four steps for dealing with overly demanding customers:

- Reread your agreement and decide whether you should comply. The benefit of the doubt should go to the client, but next time, be clear.
- Ask your client to explain his reason for the request.
- Propose a solution requiring a balanced commitment by both parties.
- Agree on the solution or refuse the request.

If you really want to ensure you never create a customer from hell, ask your own suppliers what kind of a client *you* are. And walk away from unproductive, unprofitable associations. Life is too short to stay in bad relationships, especially if you helped create them.

Sell value in a down economy

When the economy experiences a downturn, our instinct is to stick our heads in the sand and wait for the sun to come out tomorrow. What a waste! If we are committed to setting and meeting customer expectations, we must understand how customer needs change during a downturn. Let's see it as an opportunity.

During slumps, businesses become preoccupied with cutting back and preserving the status quo, so those of us who sell to businesses must wait longer for them to commit, and then they typically restrict purchases to those that reduce immediate pain. What's a business owner to do? It's time to sell aspirin instead of vitamins. In other words, you can get the edge on your competitors by repackaging and repositioning your products or services to deliver reduced costs and greater efficiency. Show prospects how your business can help them save costs and reduce risk. This is possible even in "vitamin" industries—professional services such as legal, training, and accounting; direct marketing, advertising, and PR; wholesale and distribution; and motivational and incentive providers—which sell opportunity.

Talk about preserving market share and stopping revenue erosion. While leaders are telling their staff to cut costs, they need to protect their own revenue forecasts, and it's harder to reduce a sales goal than to cut expenses. Pull out the list of features, advantages, and benefits you have developed for your products and services and revise them for the new reality. Practicality, cost efficiency, and reliability are the buzzwords for customers in protection mode.

When customers are focused on reducing risk, help them to keep what they already have. Customer retention is critical during hard economic times because existing business is more profitable than new accounts. If necessary, modify your product or service to enhance your customers' ability to keep their customers. For example, you might:

- Streamline their reordering process.
- Take cost out of how they serve existing customers.
- Improve the buying experience of their current customers.
- Increase profit margins and sales to reordering customers.
- Construct barriers that reduce their customers' desires or ability to switch suppliers.

In lean times, don't be surprised if your competitors go after your customers aggressively. Helping your customers ride out the storm is the best way to keep them loyal.

Delivery in the 21st century

If you run a manufacturing company, delivery and fulfillment may keep you in business. Far East competitors have an enormous advantage over U.S. firms in terms of labor costs, but they are far more than a phone call away from their American customers. Rather than lamenting the cruel nature of capitalism, American producers must rethink how to deliver their Best and Highest Use. Unfortunately, too many companies are sticking to the old rules. Here is a prime example. In the current fad of ISO and CS 9000/9002 and the like, many companies have bought into the magical thinking that a gold star leads to prosperity. While quality is great, any time a business fad grows faster than the federal deficit—think KANBAN, just-in-time, quality circles, lean manufacturing—you can be sure that a few people are getting fat at the expense of the many.

ISO 9002 is designed to give purchasing departments of large Tier 1 and Tier 2 manufacturers a Good Housekeeping seal to prove they have reduced supplier risk and met their bosses' objectives. Under the law of unintended consequences, however, it turns manufacturers into better-qualified providers of commodities at a time when buyers can get similar products at a much lower price by looking overseas. The latest version of ISO emphasizes customer satisfaction, but if price is the only thing that satisfies the marketplace, *how can you win*? I'm not condemning ISO consultants or practices, merely pointing out that while companies pursue the latest mythical definition of perfection, their customers are turning to less-perfect Asian suppliers whose prices are *bargain basement.*

The situation is dire for small manufacturers, who risk being driven down to bankruptcy. Contrary to reports, however, American manufacturing is not dead. Many companies succeed through innovation. They are:

- Competing in niche markets.
- Providing very fast delivery overseas competitors can't match.
- Finding customers who will pay for value.

Successful manufacturers provide real products and real services to real customers for real money. They resolve real problems and create real opportunities to serve their market. A manufacturer might focus on small but profitable niche markets. For example, a maker of stone and marble home products eliminates his low-end line in favor of designing, producing, and installing high-end kitchens for affluent homeowners and prestigious builders. A factory owner whose market is shifting toward Chinese commodities begins charging high-end customers for value-added services they used to get for free. Phoenix Products, a client that assembles and distributes water delivery systems (faucets) for manufactured housing, is thriving in an increasingly price-conscious market. Among its innovations, Phoenix has partnered with a Chinese manufacturer to sell a new line that blends low price and sophisticated design.

If you are a manufacturer, now is the time to inoculate your business. Look for ways to enhance the value you provide to customers, perhaps through creating tiers of service or repositioning your company in the marketplace. And remember that value is in the eye of the customer. Give them what they want, no more and no less, and if it fails to keep them loyal or pad your profits, forget about it.

Growing to the next level

Now that company sales surpass $5 million, your firm is the envy of its smaller peers. The CEO of your largest competitor probably knows your name and more, because you are a rising star on his radar screen. So, why does it feel as if you are starting over?

The growing pains discussed in the previous chapter often intensify at this point and may be accompanied by hormone swings. I hate to say it, but you are now in the adolescence of business growth. Yours is not a small business anymore, but it isn't a multi-national corporation, either. You are middle-market, my friend. Welcome to freshman year!

Are you happy? Are you still hungry? Do you long for the days when you and your spouse had to dip into your wallets to make payroll? Or do you still have the passion to grow?

You know you have the growth-oriented mindset when you possess the following:

- A commitment to professionalize your firm, even if it costs you in terms of ego, control, or prestige.
- The will to walk away from the company to allow it to grow, if your leadership has reached its limits.
- A sense of urgency to grow the business, even in the face of its continued success.
- A management group that is capable and hungry and can do it with or without your involvement.
- A yearning to exploit all the hard earned gains.

Just as no sane person wants to stay an adolescent, few business owners are content at this level. Some prize control over growth and want to move back into the ranks of small companies. If you feel disconnected from the activities you once loved, it may time for you to consider selling part or all of the business. If you aren't happy with where you are but can't commit to splitting the company or walking away, set a deadline for yourself to make a decision one way or the other. When that date arrives, you must choose whether or not to grow. If you still aren't sure, this ambivalence is your decision.

Your passion has brought you this far, and if it is still flaming, you are ready to grow to the next level. Only by setting your ego aside can you grow your business to become a champion of your marketplace. You are well on your way!

Client case study: Ashtabula Rubber

When Nick Jammal joined Ashtabula Rubber in 1978, he stepped right into a family tradition. In 1951, his grandfather, N.J. Jammal, had

Birol's bit: You want me to warranty what?

Manufacturers and distributors break through customer ambivalence by offering warranties. But what about service providers? Can you warranty something you can't touch or see? Actually, almost any product or service can be guaranteed through a service contract if you break down what you sell in the eyes of the customer. Think about your customer's expectations and concerns in each of these areas:

- *Delivery.* When? In what form? Within what time frame? With how much notice? Guaranteeing your answers can provide a measure of comfort to your customers.
- *Performance and output.* How will the product or service meet the defined need? To what standard? With what outcome? Through whose cooperation or involvement? For example, you might attract customers willing to pay for premium service contracts if you guarantee service 24/7.
- *Be creative.* Ohio suffers the occasional earthquake, so just about anything can happen. Somebody must have insured Tiger Woods' cataract operation. Impress your customers by protecting them against strange disasters they never imagined.

Warranties and service agreements represent an opportunity to eliminate a perceived or real risk in the customers' minds. Just be sure to price your contracts to cover potential losses and profit your company. And don't offer a guarantee you aren't prepared to keep. Otherwise, the potential cost to your firm's reputation is far too high.

taken over the Hershberg Rubber Company, a supplier of hard rubber parts to the battery industry, from a friend. By 1965, when Nick's father and aunt, Joseph and Eleanor, assumed the roles of president and VP of Finance, the company was operating under the name Ashtabula Rubber Company (ARC) and flourishing in several important markets. Over the next 20 years, the company produced crucial components for a variety of machines and systems such as standby power for computers, brakes for buses and trucks, water delivery, and electrical transmission. "We did such a good job of servicing our major customers that we stood above our competition," Nick said. "As our major customers grew, so did we."

This type of success leads to a problem I see often with middle-market companies who have grown fat on a diet of potato chips. Ashtabula Rubber, after 50 years in business, had made little headway toward establishing reliable internal systems because it didn't need them. Until, suddenly, it did.

When Nick became president of ARC in 1996, globalization was rocking American business. Cost reduction became the focus for most of ARC's major customers, who faced challenges from low-priced manufacturers. Nick responded in two ways. First, ARC committed to improve efficiency and reduce its own costs through manufacturing innovation. Second, the company leveraged its technical expertise by helping customers achieve cost savings through changes in design, material, and formulations. Yet there was a limit to what the company could do. ARC supplied a lot of commodity components to customers in mature markets, where costs couldn't be slashed low enough to match Far East labor, and where customers didn't care about quality differences. Loyal customers began buying offshore, often with apologies.

When Nick brought me in, he had been struggling for a couple of years, aware that his company must change, but uncertain of what he should do. The first thing I did was to convince him that the game had changed permanently. Globalization is the new world, and we have to learn to live in it. After visiting trade shows and speaking with many of ARC's past customers, I confirmed Nick's suspicion that price was to blame. Even a revitalized sales and marketing program couldn't restore the same kind of business the company had lost.

Yet, when it came to solving a customer's unique problem through design and engineering, there was no contest. ARC demonstrated a fantastic ability to engineer technical solutions to fit a customer's need— a service you can't get offshore.

Over the course of several months, I worked with Nick and his team to realign the company so that it could meet an array of customer needs. "What evolved was our recognition that within our own four walls we were dealing with products along the entire life cycle," Nick recalled. While it couldn't compete in large-scale commodity production, ARC had the edge in the earlier stages of technical innovations and improved manufacturing. Moreover, we discovered that many of the company's biggest customers wanted ARC to manage this full spectrum, and they were willing to pay well for it.

With a clear mission to provide engineering and materials expertise when customers needed it and world market prices the rest of the time, we split business functions into three separate "companies" operating within Ashtabula Rubber. We called them A, B, and C:

- The "A" business focuses on finding business through the engineering of new applications and prototypes. This business focuses on the pioneering the future.
- The "B" business continues domestic manufacturing with reduced costs and improved margins. This business focuses on maintaining and improving the current situation.
- The "C" business seeks partnerships with Chinese producers in order to provide customers with low-cost commodities plus the security of having a "back-up" domestic manufacturer when needed.

The great thing about Ashtabula Rubber now is that they can do almost anything a customer wants and make money doing it. "We come to the table with a full array of services," Nick said, "and that helps us in seeking new customers. The beauty is that we can go into a company selling our technical and engineering expertise, but when we see the company's commodities we can pitch those as well."

Rather than lamenting the death of American industry, Nick Jammal turned the rise of Chinese manufacturing into an opportunity for his company. Improved efficiency has lowered costs and enhanced margins, profitability is up, and ARC continues to dazzle customers with its technical expertise. "If we don't stay at the forefront of production and technology," Nick said, "we have no more to offer than distributors of rubber products made overseas." The company can't beat Far East competition on price, but what it delivers to customers is the most comprehensive value of any business in its industry.

☑ Self-check: How's it growing?

Check your progress through the $5 million to $20 million phase of business growth by selecting the answers most applicable to your firm from the following choices.

1. I have a strong conviction about my company. I would describe this conviction as:
   a. *Insatiable.* We do so many things well, but there is still a lot of potential in this business.
   b. *Strong.* We are doing well—not as well as some, but better than others. I am happy with where the business is.
   c. *Justified.* Why wouldn't I be convicted? Look at my track record; no one could lead this company as well as I do, and our success speaks for itself.

2. In terms of Best and Highest Use:
   a. *I Adjust it.* We are looking at new markets and expanding our line of products and services, so our time is more valuable than ever before. Outsourcing works well for us at this stage, because we can focus more effort on leveraging what we do best.
   b. *I hang on to it.* I know my marketplace, my best customers, and my company's strengths. In fact, I don't like outsourcing. Why

spend money hiring someone to do things you can figure out for yourself?

   c. *I don't think about it.* We can do a lot of different things, and I'm not about to turn away business.

3. To find, keep, and grow customers, my staff and I:

   a. *Balance the scales.* Our sales funnels are equally full, and our profit margins are up in all three areas. We focus more than ever on delivery but without backsliding in finding, keeping, and growing customers.

   b. *Do what it takes.* We keep an eye on the sales funnels and put extra effort into whichever one is the least full. We spend a lot of time prospecting.

   c. *Manage.* The funnel thing didn't work for us. We take orders when can get them, and we're still in business, after all!

4. Delivering our products and services:

   a. *Is crucial.* My most important goal right now is to scale up production to meet growing demand. We are having success at meeting customer expectations even at this faster pace and larger volume.

   b. *Is concrete.* We have a system that works, and if customers don't like it they can choose to go elsewhere.

   c. *Is controlled.* We know what to do at each step. The person who manages delivery runs a tight ship.

5. As for repetition and consistency:

   a. *We are recognized.* Customers speak well of us. I feel comfortable making our reputation for excellence part of our brand.

   b. *We are working on it.* By limiting our customer base to those who respond well to our core product, we feel we are creating a tested system.

   c. *We're okay.* We're still in business. What else is there?

If you circled mostly "a" answers, your company is well-positioned to soar to the next level. A "b" majority indicates that your firm is stable; your choice is to strengthen its foundation to grow, to sell all or part of the company, or to try to stay at this level. A lot of "c" answers? Your business is in decline. If you have lost your passion for the business, it may be time to leave. Otherwise, you need to get back to basics and start making necessary changes.

Chapter

Who Have We Become?
Growing from $20 million to $50 million

When Bruce Springsteen released "Pink Cadillac" in 1984, his lyrics acknowledged that "folks" thought the car was "too big, used too much gas," and was "too old" to be considered a status car any longer. The Boss, of course, was taking the pulse of his generation. By the mid–1980s, and for more than a decade afterward, Baby Boomers dismissed the Cadillac brand as the car for eager Mary Kay consultants and the slow driving AARP crowd. Similar to its sister brand Oldsmobile, Cadillac had become synonymous with *old*—a once hot car cheapened by dust, rust, and the embarrassing fact that your parents liked it. Cadillac had been surpassed by younger, cooler brands. As the Boomers acquired wealth and looked around for luxury cars, they were more likely to drive off in a Lexus, Acura, or BMW. General Motors needed to reposition Cadillac in the marketplace by attracting younger buyers. In 2002, GM unveiled its "Break Through" campaign for Cadillac, a dynamic series of commercials blasting Led Zeppelin's "Rock and Roll."

The juxtaposition of establishment car and edgy rocker was just the jolt Cadillac needed. The song had made a splash back in 1965, so it immediately appealed to Baby Boomers, for whom the song lyrics resonated: "It's been a long time since I did the Stroll/Ooh, let me get it back, let me get it back." The Break Through campaign appealed to those with plenty of disposable income, but also to their kids, who saw Zeppelin as one of the signature Classic Rock bands.

Creative marketing? Sure, but GM backed it up with substance. Intrigued by the ad campaign, people took a closer look at Cadillac and saw that the boat-like, tail-finned car of old had been replaced by the Escalade, the XLR, and the CTS—in fact, an entire line of stylish, modern vehicles expressing youthful energy and speed. If only GM had started sooner, and could now carry such innovation throughout their entire product line.

Turn to pages 230-240 in the Appendix for an Owner's Exercise to help you grow your business!

Key catalyst: Repetition and consistency

Companies at the $20 million to $50 million sales level face the daunting challenge of moving from entrepreneurship to professional management. There are several risks here. One is that the business turns into the old boat-like Cadillac, too big and square to corner at full speed. Another is that the driver, like an elderly person too short to see above the dashboard, is so intent on the road directly ahead that he or she loses any sense of the horizon.

When your company's sales rise to this level, your business is big— too big to be micro-managed, too big to rely upon a single product or process, and perhaps too big to be your business much longer. The company must be nimble enough to anticipate and respond to changing customer needs and economic shifts, so expanding into additional lines of products and services and into new markets is crucial. You began developing processes for sales, marketing, and delivery back when the business was much smaller, and now the need to diversify will test how solid those systems are. Therefore, the key catalyst at this level is *repetition and consistency*. After all, as the business diversifies you will become more and more removed from many of its functions and operations, so your "control" will come in the form of the objectives, identity, and systems you and your staff have set in place.

One irony of the Zeppelin–Cadillac pairing is that Robert Plant and Jimmy Page are both long-time fans of the brand. And why not? For decades, both the car and the band have been steady sellers, stable players in their markets despite fluctuating attitudes of what's "hot" and what's not. As shown by the revitalization of the Cadillac brand, stable, and profitable growth comes from doing the *right* things over and over again, not the *same* things over and over again. Consistency sometimes requires change. In growing your business to this level, you have demonstrated your willingness to put the company's best interest ahead of your own by:

- Recognizing that the company's Best and Highest Use is bigger than the product, the customer base, or the people.
- Decreasing your influence to let the business grow.
- Committing resources to improving consistency, recurrence, predictability, and branding.
- Extending your own passion into the purpose of the company as it continues to expand.

To succeed at this level you must step back even farther. Your leadership should take on a tone of passionate objectivity as you push your people toward mastering the processes that work, expand your vision of what the company can do and diversify into new markets or product lines, and develop redundancies to protect the business. You also must recognize a hard fact, if you haven't already. The growth of your business is leading you toward the end of your leadership tenure. It's time to start thinking about a legacy.

The well-oiled machine

At a certain point, you will hit an invisible wall when your business outstrips your ability to grow it. This happens for several reasons. Sometimes owners lack the savvy and experience to manage what has become a large, diverse, complex company, while in other cases once-thriving companies begin to decline in ways that their owners can't fix. Many entrepreneurs simply lose interest, and once their passion is gone, they must relinquish the business in order to save it. Whatever the circumstance, the business will benefit from an infusion of new energy, a fresh and objective perspective, and a passion for continued growth. If you decide to leave your company in different hands, will you sell it and secure a profit? Will you choose and groom a successor able to step up as you step down? You may not face this decision in the near future. But let's face it; at some point you will be forced to leave, even if you die in the saddle at age 80! Your obligation as a business owner is to plan an endgame, whether it involves seeking a buyer or grooming a successor. Thus, your primary goal is to get all aspects of the business operating at full and efficient speed. Whatever the future holds, consistency and repetition will:

- Make the business more attractive to prospective buyers and increase the price you can ask.
- Position the business for sustained growth for as long as you choose to lead.
- Carry the company through the succession period as you transition to new leadership.

In any case, you want to make sure the company is a well-oiled machine no longer dependent on your constant involvement. How efficient and productive are your processes for finding, keeping, and growing customers? Are there any weak spots? What about delivery? What products, services, or markets could you explore to leverage more of the company's Best and Highest Use? A company at the $20 million to $50 million level of growth is headed for the stratosphere, but plenty of booster rockets will be needed to maintain height and speed. Let's consider a few.

Consistency in sales and marketing

Success in finding and keeping customers is easily measured using your sales funnels, so check for bottlenecks and implement solutions to move customers smoothly through the funnels. One great way to enhance sales effectiveness involves scheduled pricing, which is distinct from tiered pricing, which we have already discussed. While staircase pricing can encourage customer loyalty, as buyers move up from low-priced introductory packages toward higher tiers of value, each staircase may contain its own schedule developed around predictable customer behavior.

A typical chronology of pricing begins with a conversion sale, moves up to a reorder sale, and finally to an installation sale, and it has two purposes. First, you want to build relationships with customers, and second, you want to squeeze every last drop of profit while you're doing it! An effective pricing schedule will boost your company's margins. Here's why:

- The *conversion sale* entices prospects to try you out by offering a low-priced, no-commitment sampling of what your business can do. Offer a bite-sized product or service and price aggressively. As long as you break even, you stand to make it up once the relationship is established. The goal is to establish trust, so clear expectations and follow-through on delivery are crucial.

- With a *reorder sale*, your objective is to keep customers buying, deepen their loyalty to your firm, and achieve the profits you need to grow your business. You have already paid to acquire this customer by pricing the conversion sale aggressively, so you can maximize your margins through standard pricing. Continue selling the customer on value, and he or she probably won't blink at the price.

- Finally, an *installation sale* is the glue that keeps the customer stuck on your business. You are deepening loyalty one product or service at a time, and your pricing and margins for each upgrade should fall somewhere between the low of the conversion product and the high (standard price) of a reorder product. Examples include volume discounting, preferred customer specials or pricing, or anything that rewards customer loyalty in exchange for stable business.

How do you know when to move a customer from conversion to reorder to installation status? Go back to the sales funnels you created in

Chapter 3 (also located in the Appendix) and determine the logical or companion product to the one sold at each step of the retention and development funnels. If you can identify the trigger points at which an erratic buyer becomes a stable customer and then an advocate of your firm, you can price chronologically to pave the way for upcoming sales.

Surprisingly, many big entrepreneur-run businesses don't do this effectively, and I think it has something to do with an underlying embarrassment over their success. This "aw-shucks" attitude might go over with the guys at the local gas station, but it holds companies back. Don't be afraid to demand fair payment for the great things your company does. And don't be afraid to shamelessly promote your business. While employees and corporate executives take pride in talking about their company's mission, marketing, and products, if you are similar to many business owners, you shy away from seeming too prideful or self-serving. Perhaps this is because we owners are indistinguishable from our firms. Sharing our good business news feels too much like prancing down a crowded beach belting out "I'm too sexy for my shirt." Yet, don't you have a right—even an obligation—to proclaim your growing track record using all available media? When your business is at the $20 million to $50 million level, a lot of people are depending on its continued success. Don't let them down. You have earned the trust of customers, suppliers, and employees. Marketing your firm's consistency is simply a matter of extending and leveraging this trust.

Diversifying the right way

One of the most memorable scenes in children's movies happens about halfway through *Willy Wonka and the Chocolate Factory* when the obnoxious, gum-chewing Violet Beauregarde grabs a forbidden piece of gum and stuffs it in her mouth. The gum, as Wonka explains, offers all the flavors of a full-course meal but is still in the development stage. The girl describes the exquisite flavors exploding across her tongue as she chews and chews, but when she gets to dessert—blueberry pie—her skin begins puffing out and turning blue. Violet ends up as a human blueberry, purplish and enormously round, and the Oompa Loompas roll her away.

This can be a lesson for all, regardless of age, about the dangers of the wrong kind of growth. Greed as a motivation is fine as long as you don't go around grabbing at whatever is available to turn a quick buck. Expanding into new product lines and/or new markets is risky, and it can weaken your business if it strays from the company's BHU. Staying focused on BHU includes knowing when something is not working and deciding what to do about it. How many times have you seen a company launch a new product, service, or sales initiative with great fanfare only to wait for results? While you don't want to cut off a promising effort prematurely, you don't want to keep throwing money, time, and other resources into a venture that falls short of expectations. Making the decision to pull back is tough, and the unanswered questions can drive you nuts. Do we have the right product or service? Have we positioned it correctly? Are we packaging, promoting, and pricing it correctly for this market? Do we even have the right market? Your staff can help you find answers, but only you can make the final decision to reinvest or cut your losses. Without historical data, you can't rely entirely on breakeven analysis and return on investment tools. There are too many unknowns.

Before you decide one way or the other, give the initiative a chance. Did you or your team set specific, measurable objectives, and if so, are these goals realistic? Many good ideas fail (or seem to fail) because expectations weren't set, agreed upon, and met. In sales and marketing, forecasts may be based on market ignorance or under-funding based on the need to limit risk. Is your goal to find, keep, or grow more customers? To create more leads, reorders, or referrals? The more specific your objective, the easier it will be to measure actual results.

Consider whether you have the right mix of vision and muscle assigned to the project. Pair "idea people" with people who know how to get actual results, and ask them to produce a model for success. Finally, set up a field test with a deadline. Stack the deck in one of the following ways: pick a great sales territory, a simple product version, or a traditional sales tactic and test your initiative on a small scale. Set your deadline according to a certain time period or a defined reaction by the marketplace; this is the finish line. If you experience instant success or instant failure, sit tight and see what happens. If results are middling, either adjust and test again, or scrap it altogether. The value of small-scale tests is that they force a decision. They should not take longer than two or three months, and in Internet time they may occur more quickly. Sometimes it's better to cancel a promising initiative than to watch it malinger. And maybe the idea isn't all bad; perhaps it's just not the right time.

To grow or go?

Your business is succeeding, perhaps beyond your expectations. So why would you consider leaving now? Whether it happens when sales reach $5 million, $15 million, or $50 million, at some point you will step back from your company. What are your options?

If you decide to go:
1. Sell your business and secure any profits.
2. Split the company and reinvest to grow the part you keep.
3. Grow your business through a succession or transition.

If you decide to grow:
1. Refocus to grow, if necessary.
2. Accelerate growth, if possible.
3. Buy another business and instantly expand.

For many owners, leaving is the hardest decision to make. You have invested time, energy, money, and plenty of emotion and you may be afraid of making the wrong choice. What if you choose to grow and the market falls out from under you? What if you sell and the market takes off? Sometimes circumstances force your hand. If stockholders, bankers, or lawyers become involved, the choice may be made for you. In most cases, however, circumstances are less compelling. It's up to you to accurately read the subtle signs.

You know its time to make a change when:

- You aren't happy.
- You are working harder for less reward.
- The old ways aren't working.

If you are dissatisfied with your lifestyle, scrambling to figure out dramatic changes in your marketplace, or simply losing ground without knowing why, its time to make a change. This happens all the time. Manufacturers, priced out of the marketplace they helped create, must restructure, move overseas, or move on. Small media companies, losing ad money to the Internet, cable TV, and others, must sell out to cash-rich corporations or come up with new sources of revenue to stay independent. The VCR repair guy on your corner must learn to fix DVD players and Blackberries or leave the business to his grandson, who's already an expert.

Whatever your situation, base the decision to grow or sell on the following criteria:

- *Your passion:* How enthusiastic are you about your business? What's your gut feeling about the future? If you aren't sure, flip a coin when "heads" means sell and "tails" means grow. Whichever side comes up, your gut will react instantly. Does your stomach sink when you see Lincoln's profile? Then you still have a passion for your business.
- *Your level of caring:* If you are no longer interested in your employees, customers, partners, or other stakeholders, or if you feel bound to them by guilt, you have your answer.
- *Your confidence.* Do you believe that the rewards of growing the business outweigh the potential risks? Remember, a lack of conviction can sink a business, no matter how big it is.
- *Your expectations.* If your dreams for the business have been met, have you set new goals? Are you satisfied, maybe even a little bored? Or do you dream of someday leading your industry and your community?

For each category, score yourself either high or low. Then consult the following chart:

Consideration	High	Low
Passion	Grow	Go
Caring	Grow	Go
Confidence	Grow	Go
Expectations	Grow	Go

If "grow" outweighs the "go," or vice versa, you have your answer. If your answers are mixed, use them as a springboard to examine the pros and cons of all your options.

Your responses should give an indication of where these criteria work together. If you are passionate about your business, you probably have confidence that you can grow it. If, on the other hand, your responses are mixed, look for clues as to why. For example, if you scored high in passion and confidence but low on caring and expectations, perhaps you need to look at your employees or how you build relationships with customers. Find out what's standing in your way.

Cashing out

Your passion is gone. Despite cash reserves and solid sales, you aren't having fun anymore. You feel drained, and your dissatisfaction has begun to trickle down through the rest of you company. You feel too old, too tired, too hesitant, or too ready to move on to new adventures to keep investing in a business you don't love. It may be time to look for a buyer, cash out, and let go.

First, you need to figure out what the company is worth. Do you know the present value of cash flows after taxes, adjusted for risks? Your business must have a track record of profitability if you wish to sell for a significant value, and it's always better to sell on an upward trend. Call an appraiser and find out what you stand to gain (or lose) by selling. This will help you set a fair price and have a basis for countering low offers. Buyers need to see how well your business can run without you, so make yourself dispensable as much as possible.

Where can you find potential buyers? Trade shows are a great place to spread the word that you are entertaining offers. Call your closest advisors and let them know, as well. They may be able to help you find a good buyer and smooth the transition you are about to make.

Finally, have an idea of what you will do next. Are you ready for retirement, or raring to start another company? If you simply want to feel like an entrepreneur again, consider selling off only part of your business and investing your profits into growing the rest.

Developing a plan for succession or transition

Your business is entering a new phase, and so are you. Perhaps it is growing and you're ready to let go, or sales are slowing. You want to leave the company in good hands, and you want it to be strong. How can you choose and groom a new leader, preserve the character of your business, and transition away from the company? We will examine how to do this in Chapter 10, which focuses on issues of succession.

Deciding to grow

You want to grow your business, and you believe you are up to the task. Is this realistic? Examine your company with a critical eye. Sales are up, sure, but how healthy are revenues? How much will you need to spend to grow? Can you afford it? Do you have a way to finance growth? How much risk does it involve?

Birol's bit: Grow organically...

Like professional athletes shooting up steroids to gain fame and fortune, businesses often look for shortcuts. Product quality or delivery is slipping, customer service efforts are uninspired, and core customers are looking elsewhere. When the owner finally wakes up and smells the crisis, he or she has two choices:

- Address the problems, commit to fixing them, and grow the core business organically.
- Seek artificially-enhanced growth through mergers and acquisitions.

Organic growth results naturally when you achieve excellence, and excellence doesn't come cheap. It requires honesty, conviction, commitment, patience, and tough choices. With so much at stake, many owners seek the thrill of new conquests. So, what happens? If the urge to merge is stymied, the owner has wasted time and energy while neglecting the core business. If, on the other hand, he or she manages to wrangle a deal, it may be at the expense of the firm's long-term health. He or she now owns *two* dysfunctional companies!

Mergers, roll-ups, and acquisitions are no magic cure-all. If both companies aren't healthy, "steroid growth" can carry hazardous side-effects. How do you know when your company is strong enough to annex other organizations? When is it better to roll up your sleeves and do the hard work necessary for sustained, organic growth? Despite the thrill of the hunt, you know you should go organic when:

- You have problems which require your full attention.
- Your core business has negative cash flow.
- Your business is unprofitable for any reason other than insufficient volume.

Birol's bit: ...Or get juiced?

On the other hand, if your business generates its energy from good, all-natural sources, the right supplement can leverage its core competencies. Consider turning to outside sources of growth when:

- Your core market is saturated.
- You can't meet demand outside of your core territories.
- The marketplace demands that additional services and/or new products be bundled with your current offerings. Rather than make them yourself, why not buy a company that does?
- You have created a solid infrastructure, technology, or capability but need additional capacity.

The bottom line? Buy another company only to create more of a good thing. If your products or services are weak, you can't restore them through acquisition. But if your business is solid, consider buying more customers, expanding capability, and adding products or services.

Sooner or later, you will get a call from someone who can't wait to tell you how much money you can make by becoming a mini-mogul. From strategic roll ups to creative asset financing, there are a million ways to do the wrong thing. For most businesses, the best choice is to build excellence from within.

Strive for organic growth at a rate of 10 to 20 percent per year. Know your marketplace, serve your customers, and refine your firm's BHU. This will give you all the juice your company needs.

If your heart and head are in the game but the business is trending downward, the company will need cash and possibly new leadership. This is called *turnaround* or *workout*, and once creditors catch the scent, they will swarm. They will also want to make decisions for you. You still can grow but at a high cost, such as pledging your house for a cash infusion.

Perhaps the stakes aren't quite this high. You still face more pain than opportunity, and you still feel passionate about your company, but business is falling off. You can't waste resources trying solutions that may not work. Is your BHU misapplied? Has your company kept up with marketplace changes? Do you deliver too much value for too low a price, or vice versa? You need to refocus to grow. Getting a fresh perspective at this point can reinvigorate your business. Find a consultant to help you reorganize to grow more profitably.

What if your cash and passion are plentiful and your growth is okay? Opportunity abounds, so now is the time to stimulate your thinking and execute new strategies. Refine your BHU to exploit changes in your marketplace, achieve market leadership, set your own prices, and define your competition on your own terms.

Buying an existing business

Your passion, cash, and ability are driving your success but you feel hemmed in by your own four walls. It's time for more challenge. Expand your company through a merger or acquisition, but make sure both companies are stable and compatible with respect to BHU.

To acquire another business, find someone who can manage the details. Be honest about the abilities necessary to expand through merger or acquisition, and hire someone to fill in your gaps. An objective assessment and outside expertise can help you make sense of that smell of change that's in the air, and focus you on the next crucial step toward business growth.

Case study: New England Business Service

In the late 1980s, I had the opportunity to work for a great company called New England Business Service, or NEBS. At the age of 29, I was given responsibility for the $40 million Retailer Market Division, which sold customized business forms to more than 250,000 customers, with another 1.2 million prospective Mom and Pop stores across the country. NEBS was a conservative Yankee company founded by a brilliant man, Richard Rhoades. He had figured out how to "crash imprint" or personalize the standard, triplicate sales invoice, purchase order, and company check, and then learned how to sell it through direct mail.

This seemingly small innovation helped legitimize and formalize millions of VSBs (Very Small Businesses) all across North America by giving them a reliable source of sequentially numbered business forms, a simple yet professional way to get their customers to pay bills. Rhoades and his brother went from selling business forms out of the back of their cars to being pioneers of direct marketing, customizing 40,000 orders a week and providing legendary customer service. If a city or region experienced a natural disaster, such as a flood or tornado, every NEBS customer automatically received a free order of business forms so they could keep selling and billing their customers. This earned NEBS the loyalty of millions of VSBs. It also made NEBS and the Rhoades family very successful.

I had the privilege of running a portion of Richard Rhoades' business in the twilight of his career. Even then he made his influence known. Four times a year, as a Market Manager, I led my team through the daunting task of conducting what was known as "Mail Planning." For the Retail Market, this meant deciding how to divvy up over 12 million pieces of mail featuring our 3,000 retailer-bound products on some 3,500 flyers. As we mailed to more than 30 subcategories of retailers, such as florists, hardware stores, bookstores, and so on. This was a major task, one that pushed us into using then-groundbreaking technologies like CRM systems, which were in their infancy at the time.

We did, however, use two methodologies that were simple in concept but Herculean to implement. First, we divided all our sales up into conversion, reorder, and installation sales. By doing this we were able to learn which products we should use to convert a first time buyer and then which companion or next logical products we should attempt to install on an existing customer.

We then used a process called RFM or "Recency, Frequency, and Monetary" value to segment our customers into categories and rank their relative value to NEBS. Those customers who had bought most recently, most often, and spent the most were at the top of the heap and got the most direct mail, while those who hadn't bought much in a while were at the bottom.

Intellectually this was great stuff. Practically it was a nightmare, resembling what air traffic control at O'Hare Airport would look like if there were no computers and all the information was on white sheets taped to windows. The room we used was dubbed the "war room" and we holed up in it for three days four times a year, not leaving until we were sure that our 12 million pieces of mail had been optimally planned to generate sales.

In the middle of the third day of this withering exercise, Richard Rhoades strolled in and asked, "So, how are you spending my money?" As my team and I started explaining, he looked around the room. "Replace 10 percent of the letters to prospects with 8 percent more catalogs to customers and you will be fine." Then he left.

In this brief exchange, Richard Rhoades, who had certainly earned the right to retire, kept his fingerprint on his company, passed on his wisdom, and made sure we grew sales 5 percent that quarter while mailing 10 percent fewer catalogs and increasing gross margins by 2 percent.

☑ Self-check: How's it growing?

Check your progress through the $20 million to $50 million phase of business growth by selecting the answers most applicable to your firm from the choices below.

1. I have a strong conviction about my company. I would describe this conviction as:
    a. *Complicated.* Investors, family members, top managers—everyone has an opinion or demand about what I should do next.
    b. *Unlimited.* Obviously I don't know everything, so I am committed to bringing in the talent necessary to manage our growth. In terms of the company's potential, I see no end in sight.
    c. *Required.* People are counting on me. I need to hang on a little longer until the next generation is ready to step up.

2. In terms of Best and Highest Use:
    a. *I don't think about it.* I know my market, my customers, and my company's strengths, but holding on to our foundation is tough when everyone wants to give me advice about what to do next.
    b. *I extend it.* We are excited about the new products and services we are developing, and we think the market will be excited, too.
    c. *I don't think about it.* We can do a lot of different things, and I'm not about to turn away business.

3. To find, keep, and grow customers, my staff and I:
    a. *Are on auto-pilot.* Our customers love us, so keeping them is a breeze. Acquisition and development have fallen off a little bit, but sales are steady.
    b. *Are consistent.* The functions operate independently now but with terrific efficiency.
    c. *Manage.* The funnel thing didn't work for us. We take orders when can get them, and we're still in business, after all!

4. Delivering our products and services:
    a. *Is efficient.* We are consistent, customers are satisfied, and our costs are relatively stable.
    b. *Is consistent.* We are reaching higher levels of efficiency through ISO and new product development. Costs are dropping.

    c. *Is costly.* We've had to cut back because of costs, but I refuse to buy parts from China. Customers need to understand what we are up against and cut us some slack.

5. As for repetition and consistency:
    a. *It is in flux.* We've taken some risks lately to grow, but with mixed results.
    b. *It drives our growth.* This business has become a smooth operator. The next quarter is in the bag—we're looking at our options long-term.
    c. *It isn't there.* We've had some major obstacles lately, and customers have noticed. I'm afraid of what this is doing to our brand.

If you circled mostly "a" answers, your firm is stable so your options are growth acceleration, succession planning, or selling all or part of the business. A "b" majority indicates that your company is firing on all cylinders and is well-positioned for continued growth. A lot of "c" answers? Your business is in decline—and you may be part of the problem. Refocus to grow, look for a buyer, or choose a successor, but do something quickly. The business needs to get back to basics and focus on profits.

Chapter 10

Times Are Changing:
Succession and transition

At a 2003 concert in Memphis, the female opening act threw up backstage before striding out to wow the crowd. A simple case of stage fright? Sure—if her last name wasn't Presley.

Stepping out of the shadows of the original and ultimate Rock & Roll Star, Lisa Marie Presley played her father's hometown stage shortly after the release of her first album. In just a few years, she has managed to satisfy, for the most part, the curiosity of millions of Elvis fans and is creating a fan base of her own. Her first album went gold and her second, titled *Now What*, has been well-received by critics and viewers of the TV hit *Desperate Housewives*, which uses Lisa's cover of Don Henley's "Dirty Laundry" in its cheeky promos. What is most interesting about Lisa Marie's decision to forge a music career, aside from the sheer guts in inviting comparisons with her father, is the way she is blending her identities as singer and heir to the Elvis throne. In the recording studio she is an entrepreneur, distinguishing herself from the grace and gentleness of her famous mother with tough, almost caustic lyrics, and guarding her autonomy in a way her father never managed to do. Lisa Marie controlled Elvis Presley Enterprises for more than a decade, and when her decision to sell 85 percent of the corporation to a management company in 2004 proved controversial, she cited her own limitations as her motivation. Calling it "personally a hard decision," she admitted that she needed a partner with more professional experience to oversee the $40 million organization and grow her father's legacy to the next level.

While the entire world isn't taking your measure, the eyes of your employees, customers, vendors, family, friends, and competitors are on you as keenly as those of the fans in Memphis that night, except that unlike Lisa Marie, you aren't taking the stage, but preparing to step into the wings. Whether you are retiring, selling the company, or handing it over to the next generation of leadership, the transitional period represents a risky time in the life of your business. As an entrepreneur, you have left an indelible mark on the company, and unless you have been pulling back substantially as the business grew, people who have a stake in its success will be understandably anxious about the impact of your absence. Most of us, after all, experience an element of fear and uncertainty over any major life change, whether it is something difficult like a cross-country move or loss of a family member, or something joyful such as marriage or the birth of a child. On a personal level, even if you are looking forward to retirement, you are bound to feel a sense of loss. You and your company have been synonymous, and no matter how convinced your head is that now is the time to go, your heart may have a harder time catching up. As an owner, however, your chief responsibility is to smooth the transition. Prioritize and protect your business right up to the moment you walk out the door.

Choosing a successor

What happens to a business when its passionate leader leaves? Here are a couple of horror stories:

- The founder of a small but prosperous marketing firm is ready to retire, so he sells out to a larger competitor. In just the first three months, however, more than one-third of the firm's clients pull their business. No one—not even the original owner—had recognized how vital his reputation, creativity, and enthusiasm had been to the firm's success. The founder watches in chagrin as his old employees are laid off until, finally, the new owner closes the unprofitable venture.

- The owner of a manufacturing business is stricken with cancer and quickly hands over the company to his son, who represents the third-generation of family leadership. The once thriving company has been slammed by foreign competition in recent years, requiring lay-offs and the abandonment of new product development. Stepping into his father's shoes with so little preparation, the new leader drives to his office each morning feeling ill as he counts the relatives, employees, and customers who will suffer if he fails to turn things around.

- Fifteen years after starting a small boutique with a close friend, this owner wants to cash out, but guilt keeps her from making the move. Her unhappiness leaks throughout the business, which loses momentum and sales. Finally, she is confronted by her partner in an angry exchange. The partner offers to buy her out, but the business is performing so poorly its value has slipped dramatically. The two women end up locked in the partnership and a mutual resentment until the store goes out of business six months later.

Your ultimate goal as an owner should be to develop a company that can go on without you, but who will fill your role, not merely as chief decision-maker but also in terms of spirit, drive, and conviction? If you are under pressure by relatives or other stakeholders to choose a specific person you think is wrong for the job, what are your options? And how do you prepare your successor once you know who he or she is?

A transition of leadership can shake up even strong companies, and if you are the founder or have led the business for a long time—or are just well-loved by customers and employees—it can be traumatic. If your business has not achieved an identity or brand within your market that is separate from you and your reputation, its survival may be threatened even if you promote a trusted person from within. On the other hand, an incoming leader who is an unknown quantity, as is often the case in the event of a sale or merger, is sure to unnerve your customers, vendors, and workers, at least temporarily.

Choosing the right person, then, whether as a successor you groom over time or the head of another company offering to buy you out, is essential. Whomever who bring in must be capable not only of managing the company professionally, but also of working with you to ease the transition.

Intrapreneur

While no one can replace your entrepreneurial spirit, if you have developed the right kind of corporate culture you should require some entrepreneurial qualities in your successor. If you've dined with any corporate types lately you may have heard the term "intrapreneur," one of those buzz words that come in and out of style. Intrapreneurs are "Inside Entrepreneurs" who will follow their founder's example. If necessary, think back to the early days of your company when everyone involved had the qualities of an intrapreneur: a fire in the belly, a willingness to buck convention, take risks, and do the right thing to serve the customer. How receptive is your business to this kind of resourcefulness? Has it grown a bit proper and prudish in its old age? While you want to choose a successor with entrepreneurial qualities who will keep the focus on growth, if the company culture has grown stale, you may be setting up your intrapreneur to take a fall.

Unless you promote a person who is universally respected and adored, your employees, and perhaps your customers and suppliers, will appraise the new leader with a cool eye. He or she has to earn their respect, and an intrapreneur struggling against the forces of mediocrity may alienate more people than he or she can win over. Ingenious and eager, intrapreneurs hold a mirror up to others, forcing them to confront what they have become. Just like a middle-aged, weekend warrior exercising after years of complacence, when a staid company tries to perform like a growth business, the picture is not very pretty.

Your role, then, is to till, fertilize, and seed the soil so your hand-chosen intrapreneur can succeed in your entrepreneurial role. Even if you have already picked your successor, encourage intrapreneurial values throughout your company by:

- *Walking your own talk.* Devote yourself to champions who have the passion, self-confidence, and conviction to buck the rest of your staff. If you believe they have the right stuff, ignore their quirks and shield them from their peers' backlash.

- *Selecting candidates with more breadth than depth.* To be a successful change agent, your successor must understand and integrate many disparate parts of a company, marketplace, and project. Think of all the hats you wear as an owner—you need someone with versatile skills and agility.

- *Picking candidates with marketplace, distribution, product, and technology expertise.* Your business doesn't need a politico or desk jockey to sustain growth. Whoever runs the company must know your market cold.

- *Rewarding "doers."* Pick passionate, dedicated, and busy people before loyal, subservient workers. Your company knows which staff gets things done.

- *Working with teams.* Together with your executive committee, top managers, and outside experts, audit and refocus your firm's Best and Highest Use around the target market it serves and the customer needs it meets. Team spirit is infectious.

Risk of Sabotage

On the other hand, there are some things you should be careful not to do at the risk of sabotaging your successor. These include:

- *Paying lip service.* Your unwillingness to invest time, money, or personal credibility will doom your intrapreneur's efforts. Nothing is more of a wet blanket than a leader who says one thing and does another.

- *Insurmountable politics.* When your executives can't look beyond their own departments to make their company work together, success is rare. The intrapreneur needs to be effective across departments.

While he or she must overcome conflicting agendas through his or her personal power.

- *A dysfunctional culture.* If the company culture is neither healthy nor changing, you may need to adjust the systems, structure, staff, and salary. You and your successor should perform this surgery together.

During the preparation phase, you will have the chance to watch your successor in action. Look for the entrepreneurial qualities of conviction, passion, and drive, and let the person know how critical these are to the long-term success of the business. (You might start by giving him a copy of this book!)

Trouble in the house

Working with family or friends can be a double-edged sword. My experiences with family businesses have run the gamut from supportive, reasonable, loving groups who can agree to disagree and put the company first, to immediate and extended families whose bickering, insults, and conflicting self-centered interests make me feel like the guidance counselor at a daycare center. As Leo Tolstoy wrote, "All happy families are alike, but each unhappy family is unhappy in its own way." In growing your business, you learned the importance of separating your personal interests from the needs of your company. But did you do it? Nothing on earth is more complex or potentially fraught than even the most average of families, and if you run a family business, your choice of successor may be particularly delicate. Here are some examples I've witnessed:

- An owner is desperate to retire but suspects the "rightful" heir to the title—his eldest son—is unprepared to take over the company. The two "agree" to appoint a professional manager from outside the company to run things and groom the son over a two-year period. Yet, a few days after the new leader takes over, the son's resentment boils over. He moves into his dad's office without telling anyone and begins making major (and arbitrary) financial decisions only to prove his power. This sabotages the new leader, of course, and shakes relationships between all the family members.

- Forced by illness into an early retirement, an owner assures his well-qualified niece that if she leaves her current position to take over the family business she will rule with a free hand. Just months into the job, however, she is derailed by her uncle's inability to stop second-guessing her critical decisions, and her mother pesters her daily to promote a cousin, who is lucky to show up to work sober. She loses all credibility with non-related employees when in exasperation she promotes the cousin and two other incompetent relatives.

- Mother and father, founders of the business, are ready to step aside for their daughter and son-in-law to take over, and the scheduled transition has been carefully planned. Relationships between family members, however, are murky. Unresolved personal issues plague the succession period. Frequent emotional outbursts, unhealthy competitiveness among siblings, and mean-spirited rumors consume everyone involved. Caught up in this drama, the firm is caught napping when sudden market shifts occur. Key non-family employees quit, and the business plunges into disarray.

Family Business

From Cain and Abel to Jimmy and Billy Carter to Michael and Fredo Corléone, personal relationships don't always mesh with professional success. Succession issues are often delicate within family companies. An heir who doesn't want to run the business feels obligated. A founder not quite ready to step down feels pressure from his sons. Siblings jockey for position to see who ends up with the most power when their generation takes the lead. The types of complications are as varied as those unhappy families themselves, but these three are common:

- *Billy Carter.* These are the hangers-on, the relatives who bide their time while expecting bloodline to secure their power. They behave in ways that are immature, incorrect, or even illegal, and no matter how supportive or instructive you have been, they seem unwilling to change. Yet, because of this person's position within the family, he or she expects to be tapped as your successor, and other relatives pressure you to do it.

- *Fredo Corleone*: This is a tough situation because, unlike Billy, Fredo has no sense of entitlement because of his name. Aware that he must work for what he wants, he has been laboring hard to impress you but failing at every turn. Fredo is simply not cut out for this. His work ethic may earn him consideration, but performance issues disqualify him from becoming your successor.
- *Cain*: He is next in line to run the company, he knows it, and he doesn't care about the work beyond the lifestyle it will afford him. He has no passion for the work, the company, the customers, or the products and services. And he gets *really, really* upset when you point out his mistakes!

In any of these situations it would be easy to pass over this person and select another successor, but how will you explain to beloved Aunt Edith that her golden child is tarnished? As much as you want to protect your family, and your place within it, you must first protect your business. Your options are to attempt to groom the problem person over time, to grant him or her a different, less powerful position that will help him save face but allow you to give leadership to a more suitable candidate, perhaps within the family, or get the person to leave the company, preferably by his or her own choice. In other words, you can:

- *Confront/Change.* Bring in an outsider, perhaps a consultant (who can take the fall for offering criticism) or employment specialist— or even a therapist, if necessary—and confront the person. Initiate a training process with careful oversight and extend the succession period as long as it takes you to feel comfortable that you can leave the business in good hands. If, after spending time and money, you know it just won't work, cut your losses and explain to your relatives and others close to the company that your efforts failed, and why. You may still engender resentment from some, but at least you have a defense.
- *Reorganize/Redeploy.* Restructure the company to accommodate his or her Best and Highest Use or, if he or she doesn't have one, create a high-level puff position which will give him or her lots of time to play golf and little influence over the firm's operations.

- *Counsel/Encourage*: In other situations we would say "fire," but with a family member or close friend, you be able to do some gentle coaxing that leads the person to quit—and be happy about it! First, examine the roots of his or her poor performance, laziness, or apathy. Some of these failings may result from the pressure to stay with the business. Legacies often have a hard time rejecting the throne, and mistakes and misbehavior are symptoms of unhappiness. If your relative or friend would be happier somewhere else, your decision is easy: send him or her off with your blessing.

Your last resort is to take a stand, get ready for the family fights, and install a better person to run the company. Hard feelings may fade over time, as the stakeholders see the wisdom of your choice.

Passing the torch

Succession can be difficult because at times of major change our emotions bubble to the surface, making the ground as unstable as the chalky crust around Old Faithful. Old resentments; new feelings of worthlessness, grief, and fear; jealousy and greed; a sense of being overly pressured or underappreciated—these are common reactions to the shifting soil, and few of us want to admit we experience such negative emotions. Add to this volatility the potential for communication problems, and everyone is caught in a maelstrom of unstated and unmet expectations, annoying intrusions and misunderstandings, diffidence (stated or silent) on the part of employees and customers, and an awful tendency, in some cases, to disintegrate into a kind of turf war.

So, who is growing the company? The solution to succession problems is intimated by the answer to that question, which should be "everyone." As the outgoing owner, you really set the tone. If you can keep your ego out of the game and focus on growth, your successor will be more likely to check his or her personal baggage at the door and follow your lead. The key to a smooth transition is *conviction*, as the outgoing owner and the incoming leader focus on what is best for the business before, during, and after the hand-off.

Ambivalence and agreement

Ambivalence, that old enemy, lurks during periods of succession, often showing up as an inattention to growth. It can take many forms, from a lack of confidence on the part of a future leader to an outgoing owner's dangerous reliance on the status quo. Your desire to accelerate growth—to improve your products and services, to grow profits, to secure loyal customers—is the spark that drives your business, and you can't afford to let it flicker.

Think of all the questions an owner must answer, all the decisions he or she must make, all the opportunities and possibilities to be considered before a strategy or vision is chosen. Now multiply by two! Let's say, for instance, that the sales and marketing team have been spending too much money to get too few customers. Do they need new database marketing software, or new distribution strategies? Should your salespeople make more cold calls, or target better prospects? What about a customer retention program, and if you get one, what should it include? What channels should you use? Do you have the right software?

Two minds may be better than one, but too many cooks can spoil a broth. Communicate with your successor, hash out your distinct visions for the company's future, and reach agreement on key points. The two of you must speak with a unified voice. Customers, employees, suppliers, competitors, analysts watching your market—everyone is looking for signs of disagreement and vulnerability. Don't give it to them.

So, how do two powerful, passionate entrepreneurs achieve consensus? Agree on this basic point: All your company's marketing, sales, and customer service efforts come down to three basic goals:

- Finding customers.
- Keeping customers.
- Growing customers.

If something doesn't help you find, keep, or grow more customers, you don't need it. Period. There is no secret code and no short cut.

Three ways to blow it

Let's say that you don't care what happens to the business after you leave—in fact, you want it to fail so that everyone will know how important you are. Here are three sure-fire strategies for sabotaging your company:

1. *Make it all about you.* It's your party and you can line your pockets if you want to. Make personal gain your ultimate goal. Let everyone know that your successor is a pale substitute for you, the real leader, and communicate your disappointment throughout your market. Trust crumbles quickly, so grab your cash and get out.

2. *Confine change to the superficial.* "Name" a successor in name only. Order new business cards, move some offices around, and then carry on business as usual. Stick around to quash any new, creative ideas the "leader" suggests. Respond to changes in the market by reinforcing the status quo.

3. *Pursue short-term opportunities.* Goose the numbers, sacrifice the firm's brand and reputation, cash out. Who cares about long-term growth? You aren't going to be there!

Messing up a transition is pretty easy if you can forget why you love your business. If, on the other hand, you want your legacy to be about more than stuffing your wallet, you need to give the new leader the power to implement a new vision. Together, the two of you can think long-term.

Tips for the outgoing leader

With the right attitude, succession can be a time of celebration. Look at your business. Congratulate yourself for its existence, a job well done!

Embrace your upcoming retirement or new adventure and honor your legacy to your company by following these steps:

- *Do your job.* Whether or not you are related, whoever is going to run your company is essentially your progeny. Bring him or her up well. Provide training on the essentials and agree on an ironclad schedule for the actual transition to occur. Whatever business problems you are entrusting to him or her must be clearly understood. Communicate these issues and ensure there are no surprises. If contingencies are likely, define them clearly. Keep your ego and your mortality out of the picture. The more selfless and humble you can be, the more you will be recognized for moving past success and into true significance. Letting go quietly, with dignity, and according to plan is the definition of leaving at the top of your game.

- *Exert authority and take responsibility.* Your final decision is to turn over authority to the one you have chosen. When others look to you for direction, direct them to your successor. Take responsibility for the past but not the present by turning over the visible signs of leadership. These certainly include spending authority, public pronouncements, and all hiring and firing.

- *Transfer assets and liabilities and don't look back.* Finally and ultimately, it is time to turn over the keys to your kingdom, bestowing the good along with the bad, the wealth along with the debt. Barring a last minute stumble by your offspring, this is your final step. Take it with grace and style and without remorse.

- *Reconcile your personal goals with the needs of your business.* Whether you are leaving the company in a state of survival, success, or significance, you must be willing to separate and let it go its own way.

- *Do whatever it takes, not just what is easy.* Understand that the business comes first. Never confuse what your business needs with who your loved ones are. Just as you would when interviewing employees, determine what your successor can do, and get outside help if your company's success requires it.

- *Be a mentor.* Encourage the continued success of your business by becoming a resource and sounding board for its new leader. In a crisis, you may even be asked to return to the business temporarily. Your trusted hand can be a great source of confidence to employees, vendors, and customers. However, do not get in the new owner's way. A mentor is not the same as a backseat driver!

Your final step is to walk into your future with the same conviction you once brought to your business. Do so with pride and dignity. Your team, your vendors, and your customers will admire your transition from *success* to *significance*. Whatever you choose to do from now on, do it with characteristic passion. After all, there is a reason you have achieved so much!

Creating a legacy

While in our personal and spiritual lives, charity is a virtue, when it comes to business, the desire to do good must be tempered by the ability to do well. One of the problems I see often with succession is the owner who is so devoted to his or her own legacy that the company's best interest is placed on the back-burner, usually unintentionally. These owners don't mean to weaken their companies, but their focus is elsewhere.

It's not that I am against charity. Giving back to the community is, for the majority of owners, a cornerstone of moving from success to significance, so as you prepare to leave your company, you should support non-profit groups or community causes. Seek out a charity that interests you and lend your talents, but do so in a way that fortifies your company's BHU. Here's an example: A distributor of disposable foodware is asked to help organize a 5K race for a local children's hospital. She could simply hand out fliers and donate paper cups, or she could take the additional step of marrying the cause to her BHU. Let's say that she proposes two extra contests for race day, one aimed at kids and one at adults. The children's challenge is to build a castle with plastic drinking cups, and the grown-ups have a pie-eating contest. The company's name gets promoted positively to every restaurant owner, retail manager, school principal, and other prospects in the crowd.

Find a cause that ties your skills to your passions and give away what you are best at doing. Find venues that are connected to the products or services you provide, and keep the focus on how your efforts benefit your company. For example, I enjoy providing consulting services *pro bono* or at reduced rates to other owners who have health problems, because I understand their situations. I can help out someone who needs it, while at the same time enhancing my firm's reputation. This may sound miserly to some, but it passes my test of being neither purely selfless nor purely selfish.

Many business owners are driven by the desire to make a positive contribution to the larger community, but you can't spread good will if you can barely afford to shop at Goodwill Industries. Don't raid or neglect your business to "do the right thing." Put prosperity first so that you will have enough resources to make a big impact for causes close to your heart. You always have the option to become a full-time volunteer, activist, or philanthropist *after* you retire.

Tips for the incoming leader

As hard as it is for an owner to leave his business, the weight of expectations on the new leader can be crushing. Your successor's job during the transition period is as crucial as your own. What should he or she be doing? Here are a few steps compatible with your own role:

- *Learn the job.* These are humbling times. Whether taking over for a parent or other relative, or coming into a company as a professional executive, the successor who begins with a quiet, observational approach, studying the owner and keeping his own ego in check, will do well. By its very nature, succession implies that the outgoing owner is mortal, and especially when a child is taking over a parent's role, his or her maturity will be scrutinized.

- *Exert authority and take responsibility.* As the owner begins distancing herself from the business, the successor must assume more and more duties, taking the initiative according to an agreed-upon timetable. When problems crop up, the successor must be accountable in order to build trust.

- *Get ready to invest.* Before the official hand-off is made, the incoming leader should discuss his vision for the company's future with the outgoing owner. Details may not be necessary, but the new leader should be thinking about how to invest in the company's future. The business will probably need sprucing up, so he or she will need to invest time, money, and energy to make it grow.

- *Reconcile personal goals with the needs of the business.* Whether the successor was born and raised for it or called in at the last minute, he or she must be honest about why he or she is taking over the business. Make it clear that if he or she doesn't have the passion to grow it, you will find someone else. Too often, the next generation lives out a professional lifetime based on guilt, duty, and blind sacrifice. Strong stewardship requires passion.

Is there a curse?

Some people think that a curse stalks family-owned businesses with the same stealth and evil as the bad luck that plagued the Boston Red Sox for generations after the lousy decision to trade Babe Ruth to the Yankees. Well, guess what—the curse is broken! Just as the Sox overcame the Curse of the Bambino, your family business can overcome the Curse of the Third Generation.

Superstition aside, family businesses are particularly vulnerable while they are being managed by the third generation of owners/operators. Department of Commerce and Small Business Administration statistics reveal that fewer than 20 percent of all businesses survive a third generation. Here is the stereotypical explanation. A founder launches and grows a successful business through determination and hard work and leaves it to an heir who either grows the business further or stabilizes revenues. When the third generation takes over, several decades have passed since the company's inception. Guess what? Times have changed. Markets, customers, production, distribution, finances, and purchasing—any or all may have changed radically. Has the company's BHU changed with them?

Often the answer is no. The business may have run its first course, and the third generation happens to be on duty when the inevitable occurs. Critical relationships that the previous generations built are probably in decay and may even cripple the company if not reinvented. So the new management faces a great challenge: either change the business, or manage it into decline. Presented in these black and white terms, the decision seems easy, but we are dealing with families here. Would you move into your parents' home, knock down half the walls, and hire a contractor to redesign the entire floor plan and an interior decorator to purchase all new furniture and decor? Imagine how hard it is for a "kid" to enact sweeping changes and redesign his elder's original plan for the business.

Tough, yes, but often necessary, and this is why succession issues account for such a large chunk of my business. Families need help coming to agreement on what the business needs, and often the new owner needs someone to "blame." I say, let it be me! If it's all Andy's idea, Mom and Pop can throw darts at my picture all they want.

Most of the time, fortunately, it doesn't come to dart throwing. A few years ago I worked with Raymond Arth, a manufacturer of faucets and water delivery supplies located in the Cleveland area. Put "Cleveland" and "manufacture" together and you get an idea of the crunch he was facing. Raymond's family had been in the industry since 1894, when his grandfather and great-uncles started a brass foundry, and had achieved success through a series of successful businesses. In 1956, Raymond's dad had founded Streamway Products, focusing on two emerging markets: manufactured housing and recreational vehicles. Streamway, an industry leader, was sold in 1977, leaving Raymond and his brother Michael with expertise in faucet production but no factory. With their brother-in-law, Kris Miller, they founded Phoenix Products and hired their dad as an engineer. Phoenix soon led the market in supplying faucets for manufactured housing and became a dominant player in the RV market as well, with the most extensive line of products among low-end faucet suppliers.

The manufactured housing market declined sharply in the late 1990s, with sales of new homes falling by two-thirds between 1999 and 2003. At this time, Asian suppliers were flooding the market with low-cost products. This was nothing new, except that for the first time the imports were of a decent quality. The premium pricing Phoenix had earned through its product quality and exceptional service eroded. After 25 years in business—four of them spent "chasing a market on the way down," as Raymond later said—Phoenix Products was at risk of becoming just another Rust Belt business with bolted doors and shuttered windows. But Raymond had spent his whole life learning this business, as his father had before him, and he was determined not to let the family tradition die.

Phoenix was in crisis. Once we began talking, I could see that Raymond was truly committed to making it work, but anxious and ambivalent about what path he should take. By reviewing the company's "total delivery"—

including order fill rates, lead time, packaging, product features, and servicing—we found a wide disparity between what customers were getting and what they were paying for. Phoenix was throwing value at its customers, and in many cases, the customers didn't really care. I told Raymond he had to stop being generous and focus on *profits*. We came up with two different options, each of which would require a new business model:

1. Focus on distribution as the company's Best and Highest Use by applying its expertise in reporting, tracking, assembling, and warehousing to new industries.
2. Focus on the core business—faucets—as the company's Best and Highest Use, but make dramatic changes to restore profitability in a tough market.

After some real soul-searching, Raymond went with his gut: making and distributing faucets. "I finally achieved that clarity and conviction," he says, "and I was handed a clear road map of what I needed to do to deliver specific results." One of the things he needed to do was to seek partnerships with Asian competitors. Raymond was very reluctant—I have met few domestic manufacturers who aren't—but he prioritized his business over his personal feelings. By combining its expertise in design and production with low Chinese labor costs, Phoenix Products has introduced a private line of inexpensive products, appealing to a whole new set of customers.

The company has dramatically cut costs as well, after Raymond undertook the agonizing step of reducing staff. Phoenix also targeted "extras" that customers didn't value and developed a fee scale for customized services and features. This "pay to play" mentality has been hard for a company whose mission is to supply excellence, but changes in the marketplace required it. The cost savings and value-added sales have allowed Phoenix to keep its prices competitive and its doors open. "We had to change our thinking," Raymond recalls. "We had to learn to deliver what today's customers want to buy without throwing in a lot of extras out of the goodness of our hearts." Through alliances, cost reductions, and a new pricing scale for value-added services and features, Raymond Arth has improved his company's profitability without raising prices, and Phoenix Products is rising again. A clear win for a third generation business owner!

Birol's bit: Tips for the incoming leader

Congratulations. You are about to be handed your predecessor's most precious offering: the business. You are about to become an entrepreneur, whether or not you think the label fits you. You didn't create this business, but you will create its future.

In track and field, relay runners must complete a clean handoff within a certain distance, called the fly zone. If the lead runner steps out of the zone before securing the baton, the team is disqualified. As you wait in the fly zone for your turn to run the business, keep the focus where it belongs:

- *Power past the handoff without colliding into other runners.* Complete your transition of power, accountability, and ownership of assets and liabilities.
- *Accept coaching and cheering from your team.* While you have the baton now, it can be lonely leading the pack, so seek out wise counsel.
- *Shuffle your team if you are losing the race.* If a member of your new team runs into trouble, ask your predecessor to fill in and temporarily do a needed job.

Do so with determination and humility. Your team, your vendors, and your customers will admire your transition from *follower* to *leader*.

Challenges

If you are the third generation of a family business, you must be aware of the challenge and the potential changes you may need to make. If you are a second generation owner ready to hand off, you need to make your successor aware of what is happening in your market. Anticipating radical changes and coming up with innovative solutions will be his or her biggest challenge, and you may be able to mentor him through it. Effective third generation owners use their own Best and Highest Use to mold and reshape their business to fit the modern marketplace. In so doing, they earn the right to see their name on the shingle.

Client case study: Wade Dynamics

A sad rule of business is that exceptional products don't guarantee business growth; otherwise, Pete Wade and his family would have been multi-millionaires long ago. When I met the Wades, their machine balancing shop was buzzing along at high speed, but it wasn't making money. Despite 40 years of expertly servicing machines for manufacturers, schools, universities, hospitals, and other major customers, Wade Dynamics wasn't growing. Pete's parents, Dennis and Denise, looked forward to retiring from their roles as company president and secretary, yet they didn't want to walk away until the business was solid.

In many ways, Wade Dynamics epitomizes the American family business. Founded in 1963 by Conward "Grandpa" Wade as a broken tool removal shop, the company doubled in size during its first year following Con's purchase of a dynamic balancing machine. In the early 1970s Con's son, Dennis, heard about the new technology of metallizing. This involved the spraying of metal powder onto the surface of a damaged or worn part for repair, thus saving the customer from buying a new part, or in some cases, a whole new machine. Realizing they could provide an essential service for customers and augment their company's capabilities, the Wades split their business between dynamic balancing and metallizing, and the company thrived for two decades. In 1994, Pete began working full-time and soon made his own mark on the business. Determined to find a metallizing technology that produced a harder, chemical-resistant coating, Pete discovered HVOF, an advanced process inspired by an F–16 jet engine that shoots metal powder at Mach–13 speed. The acceleration causes the particles to smash together and bond at microscopic levels, producing denser, harder, and more durable coatings—a machine owner's dream.

Talk about Best and Highest Use! From what I saw in 2003, Wade Dynamics had the capability to serve 100 percent of customers who walked through their door. Unfortunately, they hadn't bothered to tell the marketplace. The family had been relying on technological supremacy to attract new business rather than doing the hard work of finding, keeping, and growing customers. If Dennis and Denise wanted to ride off into the sunset anytime soon, the Wades would have to start running their shop less like an art and more like a business.

I worked with Pete, his parents, and Pete's wife Beth, the company treasurer, on proactive marketing, networking, and systematizing their efforts to find, keep, and grow customers. One of the first things we did was to create a three-year spreadsheet, noting each customer and contact name, the amount the customer spent, the nature of the job, and the actual profit they received. It was an eye-opener. Some of their "best" customers contributed very little to the company's bottom line. By focusing on profit margin, I helped the Wades develop a standard pricing system based on getting proper specifications from each customer to cut down on the risk of over-delivering their services.

We also worked a lot on customer service, which in this case meant serving the needs of the person, not just servicing his or her machine. "Caring more about the machines than the people wasn't good for business," Pete once remarked dryly. Finally, once the fundamentals were in place, we developed a succession plan. Everyone agreed to a series of actions and outcomes that will have the elder Wades retiring by 2007.

At our first meeting, the Wades committed to achieving profitability within three years—or closing the shop. Now, with systems for finding, keeping, and growing customers, improved profit margins, and a succession plan in place, no one is talking about shutting down. The future of Wade Dynamics is shaping up beautifully.

☑ **Self-check: Two directions toward a single goal**

During a succession period, outgoing owners and incoming leaders face distinct but related challenges, and by working as a team they can smooth the bumpy road ahead and perform an effective transition. You can use the following checklists—one for the predecessor and one for the successor—to set clear expectations and agree upon the responsibilities and roles you each will assume.

You are the current owner, and perhaps founder, of the company. You have chosen a successor. During the transition, your role is to provide:

☐ Counsel.
☐ Oversight.
☐ Public expressions of trust in your successor.
☐ Credibility.
☐ Credit where it is due.
☐ A back stop should problems occur.
☐ Many opportunities for your successor to succeed.
☐ Continued mentoring once you step down, if asked.
☐ Silence and distance from the company once you step down, if asked.
☐ An infectious passion for running this business.

You are the incoming leader, perhaps the son or daughter of your predecessor. You may have grown up in the business, or you may have recently arrived. During the transition, your role is to provide:

☐ A teachable attitude.
☐ Confidence, conviction, and consistency.
☐ Questions in order to understand the company.
☐ A plan that is your own, not merely an extension of the status quo.
☐ Responsibility for results.
☐ Accountability for the actions of your organization.

Closing thoughts

Whether our businesses are in transition, succession, growing organically, or through acquisition, we owners all share a common standing: Once we are recognized as business owners, we never want to go back to work for someone else. In our independence, we all belong to one club. The freedom, the affirmation, and the respect of most of those we meet is difficult to replicate in the corporate world and if so, it usually comes with strings attached. So it is not surprising that our drive to protect what we have created could be the professional equivalent of a mother's devotion to her child's well being. On one hand we fear the downside of failure while on the other we yearn for all the opportunity we could be missing.

How can we protect what we have earned, invest in new opportunities, and avoid the clear threats our businesses face at every turn? These are seemingly contradictory and torment many owners. How many times have you seen examples such as these?

- A successful security alarm company ignores the clear trend towards "smart homes" and integrated home theatre systems only to discover that these providers are now competitors as they include security alarms as part of their command and control systems.
- A maturing accountancy, searching for new services with better margins, starts offering executive search and outplacement. Instead of embracing these added services, their clients grow confused and wary, when even the partners struggle to explain why and how these different offerings work together.
- A computer cabling company moves seamlessly from connecting servers to setting up wireless connectivity. Their customers are grateful and even more loyal to their cabling company for shepherding them from obsolescence to state of the art.

In the final analysis, your role as a successful business owner may come down to two conceptual duties: *demanding more predictability of your existing business,* and ever-honing your skill in *scouting out your environment.*

You know you are demanding predictability from your existing business when you:

- Are not happy with great results until you know how they happened.
- Become intolerant of erratic swings in sales or profitability and refuse to only blame the economy, competition, suppliers, or customers for bad results.
- Demand that successful activities in your firm be repeated, rewarded and routine, while surprises become anticipated and ultimately eliminated.

You know you are becoming an expert scout of your environment when you can:

- Anticipate what your customers, employees, and vendors will demand and already have a solution that meets their needs and yours.
- Interpret the difference between what your target market says it wants and have the confidence to offer them what they need.
- Look ahead at least three months and anticipate what your business will need in terms of sales, cash, expertise, and time to meet your goals.

Owning a growing business is for most business owners the fulfillment of a life's work and dreams. When your business is growing, you feel in control of your destiny. You understand your Five Catalysts and the role they play in reaching your goals. The only step left is to keep your business growing in the right direction. Making it more predictable and scouting out your environment will get you there. Enjoy your journey, your freedom, and your growth!

Appendix

Owner's Exercise Series

I. Conviction

a. Bolting down your defining point

Take a few minutes to think about what pushed you to become or profoundly change as a business owner. Jot down your answers to the following questions so that you can refer to them later.

When and where did your defining point occur? Include any details you can recall:

_____
_____
_____
_____

Since recognizing your defining point, what do you now know and do?

_____
_____
_____
_____

Since recognizing your defining point, what do you no longer believe or do?

_____

_____

_____

_____

_____

How do you know this was your defining point? List at least five examples of your achievements and explain how your defining point made them possible.

_____

_____

_____

_____

_____

b: Replacing ambivalence with conviction

The only person who really likes change is a baby with a full diaper, and even then it stinks and there's bound to be kicking and screaming. With so much at stake and so many decisions to make, how do you decide to take a leap—and in which direction? Use the following exercise to work through any ambivalence you may have about growing your company. Whenever you have a decision to make and don't know what to do, answer the questions in each section. Do it quickly—take no more than half an hour for the entire exercise. The point here isn't to fret over your options, but to get on paper the gut-level choice you know you should make.

Clarify your problem:
Do you know what you have to decide? Describe the problem briefly.

_____

_____

_____

_____

Will your decision eliminate personal business pain? In what way?

_____

_____

_____

_____

_____

Will your decision create personal opportunity or business opportunity?
In what way?

_____

_____

_____

_____

_____

Get ready to make the decision:
Do you have all the information you need to make this decision?

_____

_____

_____

_____

Do you need anyone else's approval? Why/why not?

_____

_____

_____

_____

What is the cost of making this decision? Of not making it?

_____

_____

_____

_____

Are you ready to make your decision? If yes, then make it! If not, continue to the next section.

Identify the obstacle:
If you answered no, why do you feel you can't make a decision? Indicate all that apply and explain.

No upside to deciding?

_____

_____

_____

_____

_____

No downside to waiting?

_____

_____

_____

_____

_____

No need to decide?

_____

_____

_____

_____

_____

Too hard to implement the decision?

_____

_____

_____

_____

Don't know?

_____

_____

_____

_____

_____

<u>Find the conviction</u>:
If you are ambivalent about making a decision, why are you missing the conviction you need? (Indicate all that apply and give an example or two.)

Self-doubt?

_____

_____

_____

_____

_____

Pain of changing?

_____

_____

_____

_____

Lazy/no ambition?

_____

_____

_____

_____

_____

Irresponsibility?

_____

_____

_____

_____

_____

Fear of the unknown?

_____

_____

_____

_____

Locate the source of ambivalence:

Too proud?

_____

_____

_____

_____

Lack of experience?

_____

_____

_____

_____

Accountability?

_____

_____

_____

_____

Cost of deciding?

_____
_____
_____
_____
_____

Cost of not deciding?

_____
_____
_____
_____
_____

Being wrong before?

_____
_____
_____
_____
_____

Getting second-guessed?

_____
_____
_____
_____
_____

Procrastination/perfectionism?

_____
_____
_____
_____
_____

Track record?

_____

_____

_____

_____

_____

Don't see a solution?

_____

_____

_____

_____

_____

Clarify a defining point:
Decide how serious of a defining point you'll need to make a decision.

Financial damage?

_____

_____

_____

_____

_____

Death or illness?

_____

_____

_____

_____

_____

Harm or loss of the business?

_____

_____

_____

_____

Harm or loss of your leadership role?

_____

_____

_____

_____

_____

Decide not to wait for a crisis:
Decide when you will take action to achieve a balanced business.

How and when will you become decisive?

_____

_____

_____

_____

_____

What action steps will you take without requiring a defining moment?

_____

_____

_____

_____

Define what you need to learn.

_____

_____

_____

_____

Define whom you need to convince.

_____

_____

_____

_____

Define what you need to settle and by when.

_____

_____

_____

_____

_____

Once you get all of this down on paper, commit yourself to these action steps. While it may be easier and less frightening for you to make no decision, remember that passivity *is* a decision—it is a choice to accept mediocrity (or even failure), a choice not to grow. Once your pain of not changing is greater than your pain of changing, you will be on the path to accelerated business growth.

II. Best and Highest Use

a: Know thyself; know thy company

While some people instantly recognize and can articulate their Best and Highest Use, for most people it involves a little time and struggle. Spend some time answering the following questions:

Quickly jot down all the things you like to do, both in and outside your business.

_____

_____

_____

_____

_____

Quickly jot down all the things you are really good at doing—skills, knowledge, behaviors, and so on.

_____

_____

_____

_____

_____

Of all the things you like to do, which ones do you do especially well?

_____

_____

_____

_____

_____

Of all the things you do well, which one do you most enjoy?

_____

_____

_____

_____

Do you notice overlap between the final two lists? These are strong hints of your personal BHU. Now let's examine your company. Be sure to jot down any thoughts about your company or employees.

Define your organization's products/services.

_____

_____

_____

_____

Describe all the things your clients and customers pay you to do.

_____

_____

_____

_____

Describe all the things your clients, customers, and staff like about you.

_____

_____

_____

_____

_____

List all the things your business does well.

_____

_____

_____

_____

_____

Finally, state your organization's Mission Statement. How well does it line up with your previous answers?

_____

_____

_____

_____

_____

Reach out to other points of view. Ask your employees, vendors, and advisors all about your business. Track anything interesting. You can commission independent market and customer research, create methods of self-testing and benchmarking, and do Internet research to understand your competitors, customers, and vendors, all of whom are windows into your own BHU.

b. Taking aim

Ever try to sell prime rib to a vegetarian? If so, then you know the importance of finding the right market. In the space provided, list the names of 10 persons who buy from you, the companies they represent, adjectives defining their company culture such as "progressive/conservative or controlling/partnering," the specific products and services they buy, and their individual expectations when buying from you.

Chart 1

Buyer	Company	Culture	How did they learn about you?	Products/ Services	Expectations met?	Can they supply a referral, or become a reference?

What conclusions can you draw about the individuals to whom you sell? What common characteristics do you notice, and where do your values and company personality and those of your customers diverge? Think about how you do or do not shape and fulfill the expectations of these customers. Are you doing all you can to serve them?

c. Connect to Customers

Answer the following questions for each customer you listed in chart 1. The more precisely you can pinpoint your customers' needs, the more effective you can make your offer, thereby increasing customer loyalty.

Customer Names:

_____

_____

_____

Specific products/services this customer buys:

_____

_____

_____

_____

_____

Intended use for each product/service:

_____

_____

_____

_____

_____

Actual way(s) the customer uses each product/service:

_____

_____

_____

_____

_____

What problem does your firm solve for this customer, or what opportunity do you help them find?

_____

_____

_____

_____

_____

What does your customer value most about buying from your company?

_____

_____

_____

_____

Where else could your customer go for help solving the problem or creating opportunity?

_____

_____

_____

_____

d: Building EXPERT Relationships

This is a five-step process for building relationships in the EXPERT industry. Follow the following steps: First, make a list of everyone you know who may need your expertise.

_____

_____

_____

_____

Next, score each person according to the following scale:
- 10 points for those people who have worked with your firm.
- 5 points for those people who know someone who has worked with your firm.
- 3 points for those people who have heard of your firm.

Score them again using this scale:
- 10 points for personal friends who have supported your business.
- 5 points for business friends who have supported your business.
- 3 points for business acquaintances who have supported your business.

Add up the two scores for each name on your list. Rank the names in descending order by total number of points. Contact everyone who scored 10 or more. Initiate the exchange of information of value, describe the expertise you need or have, and repeat until you are overwhelmed!

III. Finding, keeping, and growing customers: The sales funnels

a: Build your acquisition funnel

Get started on your customer acquisition funnel by answering the following questions:

How do you define your target market? How large is this field?

_____

_____

_____

_____

Think of the individuals who buy from your company. Do they typically come from one or more departments within their firms, or hold a certain title? If so, what are they?

_____

_____

_____

_____

What are three questions you need to ask to determine whether an individual has the need, time, authority, and money to make the decision to buy from your firm?

_____

_____

_____

_____

_____

Based on your past experiences with customers, what are three or four recognizable signals a prospect gives when he or she is open to receiving a proposal or offer from your firm?

_____

_____

_____

_____

_____

Based on past experience, what are the two or three most common objections a prospect raises after he or she has reviewed your offer or proposal? How have you successfully overcome each objection? Conversely, what didn't work and why?

_____

_____

_____

_____

_____

b: Customize your acquisition sales funnel

Drawing on the information from the previous exercise, plot out your sales funnel using Chart 2.

Chart 2

Funnel Stage Defined	Your Customer Names
Suspect	
Prospect	
Qualified Prospect	
Developed Prospect	
Buyer	

c: Planning profitable tactics and initiatives

Your marketing communication and sales promotional tools will be most powerful when they are integrated into your sales funnel. To get a sense of what you need at each stage of the funnel, complete Chart 3. Under the "promotional tools" section, make sure to consider any or all of these channels: advertising, public relations, direct marketing, trade shows, telemarketing, sales force, customer service, newsletters, and customer retention. Consider the tangible materials you will need at each funnel stage.

Once your firm has implemented these tactics or initiatives, use Chart 4 to measure the desired results against the actual response you get in your marketplace. Create a column entitled "Actual Results" and check on the success of your promotions versus the expectations you had formed.

Chart 3

Funnel Stage	Tactics or Initiative	Materials	Costs	Desired Results
Suspect				
Prospect				
Qualified Prospect				
Developed Prospect				
Buyer				

Chart 4

Funnel Stage	Promotion	Materials	Costs	Actual Results
Suspect				
Prospect				
Qualified Prospect				
Developed Prospect				
Closed				

d: Customize your retention sales funnel

How do you turn first-time buyers into steady customers? Which of your existing customers are on the road to becoming champions? To get answers to these questions, identify the specific milestones that define a customer at each funnel stage in column 1 of Chart 5. Next, fill in the names of specific customers in column 2 of Chart 5.

The data you enter into these exercises can be transferred to a CRM program. Remember, once your system works on paper, you may want to invest in a CRM solution that, with a little customization, can handle your growing customer database.

IV.   Delivery and fulfillment

a: Stand and deliver, part I

In the far left column of Chart 7, you will see brief descriptions of customer categories, some of which are terms from the sales funnels. First, list the names of one, two, or three buyers in each category along with the companies they represent. Then, describe in detail the pain your company helps this customer resolve or the opportunity your firm helps them create. In the final column, write down the products and services that accomplish these goals along with a brief description of how the customers use them.

b: Stand and deliver, part II

Using the offers you put together in Chart 7, determine the actual and opportunity costs for your firm to deliver these packages to customers. Then consider how the offer will meet your customers' expectations. Make sure that the value you are delivering to customers in each segment is in line with the pain and opportunity you uncovered in Exercise 1, and that your firm can fulfill its promises cost-effectively.

Chart 5

Funnel Stage Defined	Your Customer Names
One-time or Win-back Buyer	
Reordering Buyer	
Stable Customer	

Chart 6

Funnel Stage Defined	Your Customer Names
Stable Customer	
Cross-sold or Up-sold Customer	
Champion or Advocate	

Chart 7

	Buyer's Name	Pain or Opportunity?	Our Offer
Developed Prospects			
First-time Buyers			
Win-back Buyers			
Reordering Buyers			
Stable Customers			
Cross-sold or Up-sold Customers			
Customers with more money than time			
Customers with more time than money			

Chart 8

	Actual Cost to Deliver	Opportunity Costs to Deliver	Customer Expectations
Offer for Developed Prospects			
Offer for First-time Buyers			
Offer for Win-back Buyers			
Offer for Reordering Buyers			
Offer for Stable Customers			
Offer for Cross-sold or Up-sold Customers			
Offer for customers with more money than time			
Offer for customers with more time than money			

c: Stand and deliver, part III

As you combine products and services into packages with distinct value and price points, make sure that your efforts are going to pay off. To complete this chart, list the features of each package (or "tier") you have developed along with your costs to deliver it, the price you have set, and the profit margin you will enjoy. Finally, think about how you will sell the value of each package to your prospects and customers.

d: Stand and deliver, part IV

Look over the charts you completed for the first three exercises. Using this information, compare the costs, margins, and customer outcomes of your current products and services against the tiered packages you have developed. If your estimates of margin gain and/or customer outcomes are less than you had hoped, rethink your packages.

Chart 9

Package Description	Delivery/ Opportunity Cost	Price/Margin		Features and Benefits

Chart 10

Current Products or Services	Price/ Margin	New Price Margin	Results for Customer

V. Repetition and consistency

a: Turning your output into value

Best and Highest Use is a rich source that can be continually mined for additional opportunities. To scale up your BHU, start by documenting all your sources of value. Think of what you produce or provide and describe the value for your customers in each of these areas:

How you sell it:

_____

_____

_____

_____

_____

How you price it:

_____

_____

_____

_____

_____

How you propose it:

_____

_____

_____

_____

_____

How you make it:

_____

_____

_____

_____

_____

How you deliver it:

_____

_____

_____

_____

_____

How you install it:

_____

_____

_____

_____

_____

How you train your customers:

_____

_____

_____

_____

_____

How you support your product or service:

_____

_____

_____

_____

_____

How you bill it:

_____

_____

_____

_____

_____

How you warranty your product or service:

_____

_____

_____

_____

_____

How you obtain reorders:

_____

_____

_____

_____

_____

How you obtain larger orders:

_____

_____

_____

_____

_____

How you obtain orders for additional products and services:

_____

_____

_____

_____

_____

How you communicate and solve problems with existing customers:

_____

_____

_____

_____

_____

How you involve your customers in guiding you to serve them further:

_____
_____
_____
_____
_____

How you ask for referrals and references:

_____
_____
_____
_____
_____

b: Meeting expectations consistently

What do customers want? There's only one sure way to find out—ask them! Better yet, send in a trusted representative to do the asking for you. (Generally, customers are more likely to spill the "good, bad, and ugly" to a third party.) Get answers for each of these areas: "In doing business with my firm, how do we add value, remove pain or enhance opportunity for your business as we..."

Sell and market our products or services?

_____
_____
_____
_____

Price our products or services?

_____
_____
_____
_____

Propose our products or services?

_____

_____

_____

_____

_____

Produce your order or provide our services?

_____

_____

_____

_____

_____

Deliver our products or services to you?

_____

_____

_____

_____

_____

Set up our products or services for you?

_____

_____

_____

_____

_____

Train you on using our products or services?

_____

_____

_____

_____

Support our product or service?

_____

_____

_____

_____

_____

Bill you?

_____

_____

_____

_____

Warranty our product or service?

_____

_____

_____

_____

Obtain reorders?

_____

_____

_____

_____

Obtain larger orders?

_____

_____

_____

_____

Obtain orders for additional products and services?

_____

_____

_____

_____

_____

Communicate and solve problems with you?

_____

_____

_____

_____

_____

Involve you in guiding us to serve you further?

_____

_____

_____

_____

_____

Ask you for referrals and references?

_____

_____

_____

_____

_____

Press your customers for specific answers (or ask your rep to do the same) and assure them that your desire to know will lead to better value for them.

c: Matching your value to what customers need and want

Using the information you gathered in the previous exercises, now write down every example of value you and your customer stated about your business in Chart 11. This chart will allow you to see at a glance whether you and your customers define *value* the same way.

Where you wrote down the same thing, you and your customer agree on your Best and Highest Use. Consider raising your prices or developing another product or service that emphasizes this.

Where your customer gave an example that you did not list, immediately focus on delivering it! (Your customer cares more about this than you do.) Perhaps you can develop a new product or re-price an existing service to make it more profitable and important to you.

Where you gave an example that your customer did not list, ask yourself why. Are you investing scarce resources to be good at something that is irrelevant to your customer? On the other hand, maybe your customer does not understand what you are doing. Either way, you have a problem to solve!

Chart 11

Area of Value	Examples You Both Give	Examples Only Customer Gives	Examples Only You Give
Sell and Market			
Price			
Propose			
Produce			
Deliver			
Set Up			
Train			
Support			

Chart 11 (*continued*)

Area of Value	Examples You Both Give	Examples Only Customer Gives	Examples Only You Give
Billing			
Warranty			
Reorder			
Larger Orders			
Additional Products and Services			
Communicate and Solve Problems			
Involve Customers			
Ask for Referrals and References			

d: Ready! Set! Go!

Whether you are trying to close a prospect or up sell a customer, timing is everything. Use chart 12 to identify which of your products and services match your firm's milestones.

Chart 12

Type of Product or Service	Milestone	What Your Firm Can Offer
Conversion	Converts prospects into first time buyers.	
Reorder	Prompts first time buyers to become stable customers	
Sell or Cross-Sell	Expands relationships by adding new products or services	
Installation	Deepens dependence and loyalty.	

Index

About the Author

A consultant, coach, author, and speaker, Andy Birol is a nationally recognized leader in the field of business growth. By focusing on the role of the owner as the "fuel" that drives a firm, he has helped more than 300 businesses clarify or discover their Best and Highest Use to achieve sustained and profitable growth. He coaches and consults owners in three major areas:

- Accelerating the growth of their companies.
- Extending their business' growth during succession and transition.
- Returning a business to profitable growth.

In December 2005, Andy's own company, Birol Growth Consulting, won its fourth straight Weatherhead 100 Award as Northeast Ohio's fastest growing single-employee business and 90th fastest growing company of any size. He was also recognized by Inside Business Magazine, which awarded him the NEO Success Award for 2005. Andy is the author of several books, including *Focus. Accomplish. Grow.*, and three titles in the *Birol Growth Consulting Owner's Series: Accelerate Your Growth*; *Growing Your Business During Succession or Transition*; and *Returning Your Business to Growth.* His columns regularly appear in dozens of publications, including *Crain's, Cool Cleveland*, and *www.entrepreneurs.about.com.*

Andy has consulted on four continents and regularly appears as America's outspoken business growth strategist in print and broadcast media. National and international audiences benefit from his analysis as a small business expert on CNN's *Dollar Signs*, and Northeast Ohioans know him as a Business Contributor for NBC's Cleveland affiliate, WKYC. His insights are regularly featured in regional and national magazines and newspapers, including the *Wall Street Journal, The New York Times, Inc. Magazine, Entrepreneur, and Fortune Small Business.*

Andy holds an MBA from Northwestern University's Kellogg School, where he graduated with concentrations in Marketing and Finance from its Four Quarter Program. He has lived and worked in Istanbul, Turkey and Nairobi, Kenya, where he served as a USAID local business consultant. He earned his BSBA *summa cum laude* from Boston University's School of Management, where he was named a Kemper Foundation Scholar and received the university's highest honor, the Scarlet Key.

Andy worked with Union Camp, Bank of Boston, and NEBS, Inc. before relocating to Cleveland in 1993 with his wife, Joan. He held executive sales and marketing management positions with Voice-Tel Enterprises and Harris InfoSource prior to founding Birol Growth Consulting in 1997. He lives in Solon, Ohio with his wife and daughter, Margo.

To learn more about the array of services Andy can offer, contact him at:

Phone: 440–349–1970
Fax: 440–349–0187
URL: *www.andybirol.com*
URL: *www.andybirolsarena.com*
Email: *abirol@andybirol.com*

And don't forget to subscribe to his free newsletter *The Best and Highest Business News* at *www.andybirol.com*.

Other Books by Andy Birol

Focus. Accomplish. Grow. The Business Owner's Guide to Growth.

Accelerating Your Growth. Insights and Examples for Exploiting Your Business' Opportunities.

Growing Your Business During Succession or Transition. Insights and Examples for Reducing Risk While Seizing Your Firm's Opportunities.

Returning Your Business to Growth. Insights and Examples for Turning Your Firm's Problems Into Profits.